Thursday, Marc

Cr
he

By Henry

A CHARIT set off on through tr next week children.

Bradley ley before leaving ary in Asia six years ago, plans to walk the entire length of Israel in 40 days.

Money raised from the trek will go to Bet Hayeled, a home in the north of the country for children who have been taken into care after being abused by their families.

The charity Kuunika Foundation, which feeds and educates 200 children in Malawi, will also benefit from the trip.

Bradley said: "Having lived in Asia for six years and working in orphanages, I could not turn my back on the children. I wanted to do something to help children get access to food, education and a loving family environment."

This is not Bradley's first trek. In 2006 he completed the 720-mile Shikoku Island Pilgrimage in Japan, braving two typhoons and sleeping under the stars.

He also trekked through the Himalayas to reach Annapurna, a climbers' base camp seated in a mountain pass at 13,780ft above sea level.

"I think the desert will be the really tough part," Bradley said. "But by the time I reach the desert, my feet will have hardened. It will be amazing to watch the sunset and experience the silence of the desert at night."

To make a donation visit www.justgiving.com/allforthekids

Fundraising mission: Bradley Cohen will walk 600 miles for charity

Walking the Israel National Trail, p. 133

Aikido Training Hall, Japan, p. 118

Teaching Buddhist monks, Laos, p. 40

Mastering Life

MOSAICA PRESS

Mastering Life

A UNIQUE GUIDEBOOK TO JEWISH ENLIGHTENMENT

RABBI DOV BER COHEN

Mosaica Press, Inc.
© Dov Ber Cohen 2019
Typeset by Brocha Mirel Strizower

ISBN-10: 1-946351-56-3
ISBN-13: 978-1-946351-56-2

All rights reserved. No part of this book may be used or reproduced or transmitted in any form or by any means, electronic or mechanical, including photocopying, recording, or by any information storage and retrieval system, without written permission from the author.

Published by:
Mosaica Press, Inc.
www.mosaicapress.com
info@mosaicapress.com

L'ILUI NISHMAT MY FRIEND

Sacha Sorrell

David ben Aryeh HaCohen

EVERY MAN DIES,
NOT EVERY MAN REALLY LIVES...

Rabbi Yitzchak Berkovits
Sanhedria HaMurchevet 113/27
Jerusalem, Israel 97707
02-5813847

יצחק שמואל הלוי ברקוביץ
ראש רשת הכוללים לינת הצדק
סנהדרי'ה המורחבת 113/27
ירושלם ת"ו

בס"ד ירושלם ת"ו, י"ג באב תשע"ח

After a quick glance at the table of contents, I could not help but devour the entire manuscript of *Mastering Life.*

Quite frankly, my first reaction was a personal feeling of having had a rather dull, deprived childhood. Growing up on the outskirts of Boro Park, my travels took me no further than Camp Agudah in the Catskills and BMG in Lakewood, NJ.

It did not take long for me to return to my senses and remember just how rich my upbringing really was. From davening at our local *shtieble*, whose congregants were holocaust survivors who came out of the camps with only their unshakable *emunah*, to the surreal experiences of the *Pesach seder,* the *Sukkah* and *Simchas Torah,* I had indeed climbed the Himalayas and higher. Having acquired the skills to unlock the volumes of Divine Wisdom, and having been introduced to the secrets of *avodas HaSHem* and *tikkun hamiddos* in my youth, I developed a mature, deep-felt relationship with The AlMighty as an adolescent. The legendary *gedolei yisroel* I got to know from up close and the endless *chessed* within the community left no room for any doubt that we had a quality of life no other civilization on the face of this planet could possible imagine.

To the dismay of many of us, we observe a generation of frum kids whose learning skills are way beyond where ours were, whose observance is far more scrupulous than even that of our ancestors, but for some reason, *HaSHem* never made it into their curriculum. This is the unfortunate reality spanning virtually all segments of frum society, from *Litaim* to *Chassidim*, including even *Sephardim* (who in previous generations were notorious for retaining passionate *emunah* even when observance was minimal.) The *shtieble* so many of us grew up with no longer exists, while *avodas HaSHem* has been pushed aside in favor of a very narrow definition of Torah scholarship.

Along with the powerful message this work has for those who were never exposed to authentic Judaism, it will hopefully reach the hearts of the observant and awaken the dormant craving for a relationship with *HaSHem*. Rabbi Dov Ber Cohen's successful search for truth and happiness can teach so many of us to appreciate the wealth of wisdom the observant Jew takes for granted and often even ignores.

May the author continue to ignite the passion for authentic Torah values among so many of our brethren, and may his own life experiences serve as inspiration to us all.

בברכה,
יצחק ברקוביץ

בס"ד

שמואל קמנצקי
Rabbi S. Kamenetsky

2018 Upland Way
Philadelphia, PA 19131

Home: 215-473-2798
Study: 215-473-1212

10 Teves 5779

Rabbi Dov Ber Cohen's book takes us on a journey of self-discovery; looking into clarifying the purpose of life and how to go about living that in a conscious, authentic and joyful way.

From secular Jews looking for meaning and spirituality in other paths, through people who were let down by a yiddishkeit that lacked the depth and connection they were seeking, to Jews walking the path of Torah observance and needing some new vitality in their daily practice; this book speaks to the minds and hearts of Jews from all backgrounds and walks of life.

Well-written, philosophically sound, intellectually stimulating and emotionally moving, this book is a breath of fresh air to those yearning for authentic Jewish philosophy, spirituality and practice.

Rabbi Dov Ber should be blessed with continued success in his own journey as well as in inspiring Yidden from across the spectrum to live an empowered, conscious and joyful Jewish life based on the wisdom and values of our Torah Sages throughout the generations.

B'hatzalacha Rabbah,

בס"ד

Rabbi Zev Leff

Rabbi of Moshav Matityahu
Rosh HaYeshiva—Yeshiva Gedola Matityahu

הרב זאב לף

מרא דאתרא מושב מתתיהו
ראש הישיבה—ישיבה גדולה מתתיהו

D.N. Modiin 71917 Tel: 08-976-1138 טל' Fax: 08-976-5326 פקס' ד.נ. מודיעין 71917

Dear Friends,

I have read portions of "Mastering Life" by Rabbi Dov Ber Cohen. The book presents a record of Rabbi Cohen's journey to becoming a Torah observant Jew. His life experiences and exposure to a myriad of lifestyles and philosophies enable him to truly appreciate the eternal truths of a Torah life and Torah values. The message he offers is that whatever he found valuable in the various other lifestyles and philosophies are already contained in Torah and the false values and ideas are totally overshadowed and negated by the truth of a Torah way of life.

Most people do not have the rich bachground of experiences to compare to Torah and not having a deep Torah foundation often feel the grass is greener in the foreign pastures of non-Jewish philosophies and life styles. Rabbi Cohen's book will enable one to discover the beauty, enlightenment, truth and superiority of a Torah way of life vicariously through the eyes of one who has experienced many other paths.

I found this book extremely interesting, informative, (The information regarding idolotrous ideas and customs are presented to either negate them in comparison to Torah or to show that if there is substance to them they are already contained in Torah in a superior manner. Hence they classify as laytzanusa of avodah zarah which is permitted reading.) entertaining, enlightening and inspiring.

I feel this account will aid those who are on a similar path, journeying towards reclaiming their spiritual heritage as Jews. However, I feel it will also benefit those never exposed to this search as they were born to Torah observant families and those who have already reached the goal of their search and journey to a Torah way of life, by giving them inspiration, by validating a Torah way of life appreciating the light by contrast to the darkness.

I commend Rabbi Cohen for a quality presentation and pray that Hashem Yisborach grant him and his family life, health and the wherewithal to continue to inspire fellow Jews.

Sincerely,
With Torah blessings

Zev Leff

Rabbi Zev Leff

Congregation Aish Kodesh of Woodmere
351 Midwood Road
Woodmere, N. Y. 11598
516 - 569-2660

RABBI MOSHE WEINBERGER

קהילת אש קודש דוודמיר

הרב משה וויינבערגער
מרא דאתרא

ב"ה

ר"ח מרחשון תשע"ט

Rebbe Nachman began to tell his remarkable tales with the words: "Along the way I told a story..." In this world each one of us has his own story. Each one of us is "along the way" trying to find purpose and meaning to our lives. Just as Bnei Yisroel were required to pass through the desert making 42 stops along the way, so it is with each and every one of us.

My dear friend R. Dov Ber Cohen has written a remarkable account of his personal journey in search of the truth. "Mastering Life" is a book filled with humor, insight, but most of all, humility. It is an inspiring testament to G-d's mysterious way of reaching out to us. Many choose to ignore His call, to run in the opposite direction. Dov Ber did not. With fascinating detours and occasional slip ups, he remains faithful to his decision to move forward. He takes us along with him and in doing so encourages us to be seekers as well, to remember the ultimate purpose of our descent into this world.

I sincerely believe that we all have much to gain from this profound, yet entertaining story of one man's relentless search for the truth of Hashem and His Torah.

Enjoy the trip!

בידידות נאמנה ואהבת נצח

משה ווינבערגער

Table of Contents

Acknowledgments

First and foremost, my Abba and Ima—truly the most loving, supportive, understanding, and sweet parents anyone could ever ask for. Everything I have ever done and who I have become is founded on the loving, healthy environment I was brought up in. You should merit to have long, happy, and healthy lives in this world and the next.

There are too many *rebbeim* to mention them all, but here are some who stand out:

Rabbi Noach Weinberg, *z"l*, for showing what real passion looks like. Rabbi Dovid Learman, for giving me my love of Gemara. Rabbi Noam Kahana, for giving me my love of real *avodah* and being a *l'chatchila* Yid. Rabbi Nachum Chaimowitz, for awakening my *penimiut*. Rabbi Moshe Zeldman—some people say, "Thank G-d for Rabbi Zeldman." I say, "Thank Rabbi Zeldman for G-d." Rabbi David Aaron, for showing me that Judaism speaks my language. Rabbi Binny Freedman, for giving me the power of stories. Rabbi Raz Hartman, for giving me *tefillah* and community. Rabbi Akiva Tatz, for being a supportive mentor and role-model educator. Rabbi Barry Klein, for teaching me how to pull apart a Gemara and put it back together again. Rabbi Aaron Leibowitz, for showing what it means to really care (and for second-day Rosh Hashanah *Mussaf*). Rabbi Mike Feuer, for making halachah a living entity. Rabbi Jamie Cowland, for being such a loving and supportive boss. Rabbi Moshe Weinberger, for opening the hearts of this generation. Rabbi Itamar Schwartz, whose *sefarim* have completely transformed my *Olam Hazeh* and *Olam Haba*.

You should all have much continued *hatzlachah* in empowering Yidden and bringing them closer to themselves and their purpose.

The donors who supported this vision and made it viable, in particular Moshe Oratz, Hila Sion, Nicole Sorrell Martin, and Michal and Ari Gruen—you should have much *shefa* in *ruchniyut* and *gashmiyut*.

The staff at Mosaica Press, especially Doron Kornbluth and Sherie Gross, for your support, patience, and commitment to my vision, and Daliya Shapiro and Meira Lawrence for your top-notch editing job!

Eishet chayil mi yimtza? Who can find a woman of valor? The truth is, me, *baruch Hashem*.

Oriana Devorah, my *eishet chayil*—peaceful Jewish warrior woman. Usually, when the husband becomes a rabbi, his wife becomes a rebbetzin. With us, it was the other way around—you were always a rebbetzin, and when I got *semichah*, I finally pulled myself up almost to your level. My best friend, partner, *zivug amiti*—you should have much *nachat* from the kids, and grow ever closer to yourself, your family, Hakadosh Baruch Hu, and Am Yisrael.

הודו לה' כי טוב כי לעולם חסדו.

טוב להודות לה' ולזמר לשמך עליון ולהגיד בבוקר חסדך ואמונתך בלילות.

Ribono Shel Olam—for giving us the Guidebook and not just showering me with blessing, but sending a whole flood! You should get much *nachat* from Your children.

Life is a great battle.[1]

This battle is not external; it is raging deep within each of us.

It's to overcome our lower nature and manifest
our Divine selves in the world,

to turn darkness into light, confusion into clarity,

challenge into growth, mediocrity into greatness.

It's a struggle to do the right thing in the face
of adversity and pressure,

to live with the right values, to perfect ourselves
and the world around us.

This battle is not fought with destructive weapons of war,
which harm ourselves, others, and the world around us;
it is fought with mindfulness and wisdom,

consciousness and joy.

The way is one of learning to find peace, clarity, direction,
and connection;

to calm the mind, develop our character traits,
and manifest our true spiritual selves

against all the odds.

We are being lovingly watched over and directed
by the One True Master;

The One who gave us the Guidebook to show us the way.

This battle is not to be feared or escaped; in fact,

it's exactly what we've been created for.

Sometimes we'll fall, sometimes we'll get knocked down;

but with passion and perseverance we will surely prevail.

It's the path to true mastery.

This, my friends, is what it means, to walk the path of the

Enlightened Jewish Master.

---

1 Rabbi Moshe Chaim Luzzatto (known as the Ramchal), *Mesilat Yesharim* (Path of the Just), chap. 1, "*HaMilchamah HaChazakah.*"

Introduction

"I'm with the long-haired yogi and the blankets—no sign of the donkey!"

I heard a subtle tone of anxiety edging its way out through my wife's normally soft, calm voice.

"That's fine," I replied in the most reassuring voice I could muster. "Looks like the pot, flutes, and vegetables have definitely been stolen, and three people have gone missing. I'm going to find them now and hopefully meet you in about twenty."

Possibly not the best response to ease that anxiety, but I had no time for formalities now, as we were scheduled to set off early on our expedition—with fifteen Israeli backpackers—to volunteer in a village school in the foothills of the Indian Himalayas before the oppressive midmorning heat kicked in.

Granted, it wasn't your average conversation for a recently married, newly observant Jewish couple living in the heart of Jerusalem, and certainly not one I ever thought I'd be having with my wife after supposedly "settling down." However, like so many other occasions throughout the years, I felt incredibly alive and comfortable with the situation, as the rumble of adventure began surging its way through my life once again...

You may have picked up this book because it sounds like an interesting story. While that may be so, the idea behind this book is much more than sharing what I've experienced on my journey.

It's simply not enough to be just "interesting."

The point of this book is to share the lessons I've learned, to be impactful, to stimulate a shift, and to inspire transformation. The point of this book is to encourage people to take an active role in writing their own life story in the most positive and meaningful way possible.

We all have a story. We all have lessons we've learned, struggles we've overcome, experiences that change us, insights that give us new perspectives. We're all a complex combination of thoughts, feelings, conditioning, beliefs, hopes, issues, dreams, and challenges. We're all writing and illustrating the story of our lives, moment by moment. One day we will look back and, hopefully, enjoy reading what we wrote.

We don't just have to go along with things, hanging in there, trying to make the most of our circumstances, caught up in the challenges of life—surviving rather than thriving. We can live a life of empowered wonder, depth, meaning, adventure, growth, and contribution.

My goal is to help make sure we don't let our circumstances define us or how we feel or what we do. Allow yourself to dream again, to live fully and express yourself, to love yourself for no reason. Clarify the purpose and your goals and then work toward living them—joyfully.

Let's live extraordinary lives, undertaking this magical journey together with the powerful words of Hillel in mind:

> *If I am not for me, who is for me? And if I am only for myself, what am I? And if not now, when?*[1]

Let the adventure begin.

---

1 *Pirkei Avot* 1:14.

CHAPTER 1
In the Beginning
Choosing the Path of the Enlightened Master

It was late afternoon. The shadows were beginning to lengthen across the lawn, and the evening chorus of crickets started its nightly concert. The delicate purple flowers on the jacaranda trees were melting into silhouettes against the night sky, and the smell of dinner began wafting through the hallways.

I was sitting with my grandfather in the garden of the nursing home in which he lived until his passing at one hundred years of age. Although he was confined to a wheelchair for the last few years of his life, his mind was sharp right up until the end. My grandmother had died a few years earlier, and although he had friends and family, he was left for much of the day on his own, reading books or lost in his thoughts. Breaking the silence of contemplation, he said something exceptionally powerful to me, something that shaped me and how I live, and will live, the rest of my life:

"You know, Bradley,[1] you don't want to live an 'I should have' life."

After my prompt for clarification, he continued:

"You don't want to live a life that when you get to my age, you look back and think to yourself, 'I should have traveled more, I should have told my wife more often how much I love her, I should have spent more time with friends, I should have worried less what people think of me, I shouldn't have worked so hard, I should have asked if there is a greater

1 My English name.

purpose to life.' You can make sure you live your life now in such a way that when you get to my age, you can look back in satisfaction at all the things you accomplished and experienced."

Insightful words from a man who had had a good—yet by no means easy—life and who now had time to reflect on a journey that was about to come to an end. At that moment, I fully accepted the challenge that he laid down, and I committed to take responsibility for living the greatest life possible and ending it with no regrets.

Dinner arrived, and it was time for me to leave. I gave him a kiss on the head and said, "Thank you, Grampa. I'll do my best."

> *The foundation of piety and root of all pure spiritual work is to clarify and verify what we are meant to be doing in this world.*
>
> *Mesilat Yesharim*[2]

My sister and I grew up in a thriving Reform Jewish community in North London. We went to shul most Friday nights until my bar mitzvah, had Pesach Seders, and lit Chanukah candles. I played football[3] in the Jewish Sunday league, had Friday night dinner as a family every week, and went to shul for the High Holy Days. I joined Habonim Dror youth group, did Jewish studies as an extra subject for GCSEs,[4] and I visited Israel a few times—including living on a kibbutz for three months when I was eighteen years old.

In this way, although I never considered Judaism a viable spiritual path, I was imbued with a strong enough Jewish identity that throughout my travels, even though I ate snake, lobster, buffalo, live fish, and a fine "tender and spicy" dog soup after my taekwondo black belt test in Korea,[5] I have never knowingly eaten pig; that would be going just a little too far for a nice North London Jewish boy.

---

2 *Mesilat Yesharim*, chap. 1: יסוד החסידות ושרש העבודה התמימה הוא שיתברר ויתאמת אצל האדם מה חובתו בעולמו.

3 Soccer.

4 General Certificate of Secondary Education—state exams for sixteen-year-olds.

5 They had only assured me it wasn't pig—I probably should have checked further into it before tucking in.

I had a wonderful childhood, thanks mainly to my parents. After a personal development seminar I attended, where everyone was sharing their issues, I called home to complain to my parents that they had completely ruined the course for me, having thoroughly neglected to mess me up in any way whatsoever while I was growing up. The most loving, supportive, and well-balanced parents any child could hope for, they were at almost every football, rugby, table tennis, and tennis match I ever played in, rain or shine. In addition, they schlepped my sister and me to almost every art gallery and museum in the whole of Europe, and ended up visiting me in Sri Lanka, Thailand, Korea, India, and Japan.

It's very easy to live an adventurous life like I did when one has a stable, supportive, and loving base to go back to. I remember living in villages with no electricity or running water other than the river (two kilometers away), thinking that it was the best life, free from stress and responsibilities—until I realized that it only seemed so good to me because I could just get up and leave whenever I wanted, unlike the locals, who were stuck there for the rest of their lives.

I really enjoyed school, managing to surf the borderline between "inspiring" the class and being kicked out. Although I often fell on the wrong side of the line, I generally ended up safely where I was meant to due to the fact that my grades were consistently at the higher end of the scale. Toward the end of school, I started losing my way a bit as my natural teenage spirit for adventure and experimentation began to take over. On Friday nights after Shabbat dinner, I'd make my way to The Gallery, a club near Kings Cross Station, and emerge into the sunlight eight hours later, having danced the night away to some of England's top DJs. Over the four years that I went to the five-day Glastonbury music festival (the biggest of its type in the world), I saw some of the biggest names in music—as well as a group of Hare Krishnas who sang the same mantra at an increasingly frenetic pace, nonstop for four hours. Funnily enough, that came in handy many years later when I ended up in their headquarters in Vrindavan, three hours South of New Delhi, and was able to join them in all their chants. I even dabbled a bit in being a music DJ and played in some clubs in Manchester and at the Cambridge University end-of-semester party. Despite all this, being good Jewish private-school boys at heart, my friends and I never let the music scene take over our lives. It remained a passing phase from which we all emerged (mostly) unscathed. Although I spent more time in the gym than I did studying for my A-level exams,[6] I managed to come out with respectable enough grades to get into Manchester University to study philosophy—the only thing I could think of doing at the time.

That's where things started falling apart. University was a really bad time for me. It seemed to me that most people, including myself, weren't particularly happy or empowered. We were just trying to ride the waves of the challenges life was throwing us—difficult relationships, unfulfilling jobs, messed-up value systems, stressful exams, and an overall sense of meaninglessness.

I started an existential experiment. I walked around asking people, "How are you?" The general response was along the lines of "Can't complain," "Getting by," "Not too bad," "Fine," "Hanging in there," "Could be worse," and other such lackadaisical answers. It seemed like a tragedy to me that this was the general feeling in the world I lived in. Most people didn't love their jobs, many people were suffering from depression, divorce rates had risen, and there was a widespread escape into drug use and entertainment as a means to take a break from life for a few hours, which of course, didn't help and usually made things worse. Looking toward my own future, it didn't seem too bright. What were the odds that my life would turn out any better?

Even looking at the many people who were living good, happy, and fulfilling lives, I noticed that it wasn't because they had sat down to question the purpose of life and then committed to consciously working toward that. They were just going with the flow, not asking too many questions, making the most of things, and life was going well for them. It seemed that most people just became a product of their society and upbringing, and weren't living what I call a well-thought-out life, i.e., one in which they asked themselves a) what they believe, b) why they believe it, and c) how they know they're right.

6 State exams given to eighteen year olds.

I started to wonder whether there is a greater point to it all, something beyond the surface that we are meant to be tapping into and achieving. I realized—or rather hoped—that daily life in the West couldn't be the be-all and end-all. There had to be more to life. I had a choice to fight for that goal or to go along with the flow, and that flow didn't look like it ended up anywhere particularly appealing.

I wanted to thrive, not just survive. As William Wallace said in the film *Brave Heart*, "Every man dies, not every man really lives."

At that point, I felt like I wasn't really living, and, having reached the low point of my life, I was either going to crash or dig really deep and reach really high. Like most things in life, the greater the stretch, the greater the potential for growth.[7] In my final year of university, I stopped all unhealthy habits, didn't miss one lecture, started going to the gym, meditating, doing tai chi, karate, and going for long walks in the park to find space and clarity. I started reading classic books about personal journeys[8] and most importantly, I started really *thinking*. I suddenly felt totally alive, searching for the truth, for the diamonds buried deep down somewhere just out of my reach. A note scribbled on the side of one of my lecture pads from that time reads: "My mind is getting too big for my head." It was a different sort of mind-expanding experience than the ones I was used to. Like a butterfly emerging from a cocoon, I was finally breaking out of my old thought patterns and conditioning and starting to take control of my destiny.

Like a butterfly emerging from a cocoon, I was finally breaking out of my old thought patterns and conditioning and starting to take control of my destiny.

I began spending hours in the library, reading about mysticism, Eastern philosophy, and meditation. The teachings of Buddhism resonated with me. Their ideas focused on detachment from the physical

7 Something I experienced as I was catapulted back up from the end of the 216-meter drop, having just jumped off the platform of the world's highest bungee jump, another crazy attempt to seek out life's peak experiences.

8 Including *Siddhartha* by Hermann Hesse, *Way of the Peaceful Warrior* by Dan Millman, *The Alchemist* by Paulo Coelho, and *The Celestine Prophecy* by James Redfield.

world (which causes suffering), controlling the mind (which plagues us constantly), correcting negative character traits, and generally helping us rise above life's hardships and challenges. In their view, it is impossible to be involved in this world, with its materialism, physical pleasures, and emotional trials, without it leading to suffering. Their answer is to retreat from engagement in the physical world, seeking spirituality in natural caves and secluded temples. It sounded like just what I needed.

I started watching martial arts films and saw people learning to have discipline, train their body and mind, and go beyond the normal experience of life. It was then that I started planning my "Warrior's Journey." I decided that after leaving university, I would travel the world, discover the purpose and meaning of life, and then create something based on what I'd learned. I was set on living my dreams, experiencing life and the world fully, rather than just finding a job straight away without knowing clearly what life is about and what I was living for.

In my mind at that time, all true wisdom lay to the East; in the peaks of the Himalayas, in colorful temples in the jungles of Thailand, and at the feet of old, white-bearded masters in the mountains of Japan. There I could find real sages, learn to control the mind and body, rise above the sufferings of life, and reach true mastery and enlightenment. It didn't even cross my mind to consider Judaism, which to me was at best a nice tradition yet seemed to have nothing to offer in terms of a true spiritual path.

Of course, at that time I'd never come across the likes of real Jewish masters—Rabbi Shimon Bar Yochai, the Arizal, Rambam, Ramchal, the Baal Shem Tov, Rabbi Akiva Eiger, the Vilna Gaon, Rebbe Nachman, the Chofetz Chaim, Rav Kook, the Lubavitcher Rebbe, and Rav Moshe Feinstein, to name but a few—Jews who throughout the generations blazed a path to ultimate self-realization and God-consciousness based on ancient wisdom, mindful living, authentic prayer, and deep meditation.

By the end of university, I was ready to start the real adventure of life, to set off to the Lands of the Rising Sun in search of true meaning and enlightenment. The journey of the Enlightened Jewish Master-in-training was about to begin.

CHAPTER 2

Sri Lanka

Chilling with the Elephant Man

Sri Lanka, situated just thirty-one kilometers off the southeast coast of India, is to this day one of the most vibrant, lush, tropical, warm, friendly, and culturally diverse places to which I've ever been. Oozing with ancient culture, one comes across hidden caves scattered throughout the island, displaying exquisite wall art dating back to prehistoric times, ruins of once-thriving civilizations, temples lined with ornate sculptures, and rock fortresses sprawling up into the forest-covered mountains. The landscape is breathtaking, boasting world-famous tea plantations stretching out as far as the eye can see, mile upon mile of thick rainforest that plays home to thousands of species of tropical flora and fauna, and some of the best palm-lined surfing beaches in Southeast Asia.

It was to this paradise island that I arrived on September 16, 2000, the first stop on my journey of self-discovery and a far cry from the "developed" world I had left behind. Sri Lanka was the most random place I could think of at the time; yet from the moment I arrived, I felt more at home and alive than I ever had before...

After receiving my BA honors degree in philosophy and completing a month-long intensive course in teaching English as a foreign language, I booked my one-way ticket and set off on the first leg of my epic adventure in the East. After a two-hour journey from the airport, I arrived in Kegalle, a small yet bustling town halfway between Colombo, the capital, and Kandy, the cultural center of Sri Lanka. I had never seen so many people in one place at the same time, each one going about their business, a cacophony of sounds, sights, and smells, bus and motorbike horns, street vendors calling out their wares, all interlaced with the barking of dogs, mooing of cows, and bleating of goats, which were all roaming freely around the busy streets. Although the monsoon season had officially ended, the rains were still in full force, and muddy rivers overflowed their banks, flooding the already poorly paved roads. The buses were crowded to bursting point, with people literally hanging out the doors and sitting on the roof. Yet despite this, I never saw anyone lose their temper or composure. I guess that when one is poor, there is less sense of self, less haughtiness and focus on "me and mine," of "do you know who I am-ness." Everyone is in the same creaky boat, trying to make it to shore together.

In general, Sri Lankan people are humble, unassuming, and friendly; they get on with their day-to-day life, trying to eke out a living and put food on the table, devoutly stopping in to the local temple to pray each morning and evening.

I spent a couple of weeks in Kegalle, teaching English to the staff of an agricultural co-op called Sanasa and working in the local orphanage. Although there were few other Westerners there, I felt like getting away from everything I knew, and my main pastime when I wasn't teaching was building a hut in the forest for the rubber-tapping workers to rest in during the midday heat. My tender middle-class hands, which had never seen a real day's work, were soon blistered and bleeding from the hoeing and chopping, but that didn't deter me. I ripped the sleeves off my T-shirt, tied them around my hands, and continued hacking away, much to the amusement of the locals, who, to be fair, were actually doing most of the work. I paid the price for that act of bravado for the next week or so, as it made eating a meal of hot rice and curry with my bare hands that much more painful, another good source of amusement for my new friends.

Down the road from the center was an elephant orphanage, where I used to help out and sometimes ride the elephants, which on command would take up a trunkful of water and spray it backward onto their unsuspecting rider. I soon became good friends with one of the workers there, Senerat, who was around ten years my senior and had come from Northern Sri Lanka. He was trying to make a life for himself in the central region, which had been less affected by the vicious and drawn-out civil war. He had learned English and become pretty westernized, touchingly proud of his denim jacket that he'd wear every day, whatever the weather. We used to climb up into the forests to temple ruins, where we'd sit drinking beer and comparing cultures—he'd teach me Sinhala and I'd help him with his English slang. Behind his large soft brown eyes something betrayed his difficult past, and one drunken night he shared his ordeal with me. Five years earlier, he'd seen his village in Northern Sri Lanka overrun by the LTTE,[1] who massacred much of the population, including most of his family. Apart from Senerat, just his brother, sister-in-law, and their three kids managed to escape. They were now trying to rebuild their lives somewhere near a lake in the middle of the country, living from hand to mouth, as did most Sri Lankans.

I was made acutely aware of what a cushioned and privileged life I had been blessed with, far removed from the suffering and horrors so prevalent throughout the world. Some people feel very guilty about their privileged upbringing, asking, "Why did I deserve this?" or "Why is it fair?" For me, guilt didn't seem like an appropriate feeling, seeing as I had done nothing wrong. What I did feel, though, was a tremendous *responsibility* to share my privileges with those who weren't lucky enough to be born with them.

Life is much more fully lived when the focus is not on myself but on how I can be there to improve the lives of others.

Very soon after my arrival in Sri Lanka, and possibly for the first time in my life, I realized that it's not all about me and my needs, my relationships, my dreams, my money. Life is much more fully lived when the focus is not on myself but on how I can be there to improve

1 Liberation Tigers of Tamil Eelam, a militant group fighting for independence in Northern Sri Lanka.

the lives of others. I realized just how much I have, and therefore how much I have to give.

The more one has, the more one wants.

Sri Lankan proverb

איזהו עשיר? השמח בחלקו.

Who is rich? The one who is happy with his lot.

Pirkei Avot 4:1

I left England with just nine kilograms on my back: a couple pairs of pants, some shorts, some T-shirts, underwear, and a sweater—and even that was more clothes than most of the people I was to meet on my journey had. Added to that, I had a mosquito net, a ten-meter piece of string, a head torch, writing pad, padlock, diary, mosquito spray, Swiss Army knife, toothbrush and toothpaste, painkillers, antiseptic cream, and a couple of books.

There's a saying in India, "The poor man sleeps well." He has nothing to lose. He doesn't have to worry about his car getting scratched or his stock going down. Similarly, living out of a backpack leaves you little choice: you can only carry what you really need, and it is incredibly liberating to realize just how little one needs to get by. Having limited "stuff" taught me to really value, take care of, and appreciate everything I had, as well as learn a lot about myself and what was important to me. My ten-meter piece of string was essential for putting up the mosquito net, hanging laundry up to dry, building shelters, and repairing my backpack. I valued it immensely and rolled it up and packed it away carefully each time I moved on. In Asia, insect repellent is indispensable if you want to have any peace of mind, whether walking through a jungle, meditating on a mountain, or sitting around a fire on the beach. I guess I'd add on to the Indian saying—"The poor man sleeps well...as long as he has a mosquito net."

However, for me, having very little was a choice, unlike for the people with whom I was spending the bulk of my time. From working in the orphanage in Kegalle, and time and again from the attitude of people in Sri Lanka, India, Malawi, and Thailand—who were surviving on the bare minimum of one meal a day and one set of clothing—I really learned one of the essential lessons in life and main keys to happiness: appreciation. For these people, life was certainly a struggle, but that's what made them grateful for every little thing they did have, and they seemed genuinely more content than many of my friends back home. I once bought a pencil for each of the kids in the orphanage, who until then shared one pencil between five of them. It was the most moving sight to see the joy in their eyes, the authentic wonder at having their own pencil. Every meal they received, every smile or hug or game we shared, brought so much delight to their lives and taught me that it is not what you have but rather how much you appreciate it that creates true happiness.

It seemed to me that so often I'd focus on what I didn't have, saying to myself, "If only I had a better job/car/phone/computer/relationship/more money/looked different...then I'd be happy," or, "When I'm rich/married/have kids/have more free time/get healthy...then I'll be happy." It became so obvious that focusing on what we don't have or comparing ourselves to other people who do have those things only brings us down. I decided to start focusing on and fully appreciating what I did have, and I quickly saw the positive effect this had on my life.

I soon noticed that apart from more contentment in life, this attitude has many other benefits. Not only does it breed happiness, it also helps get rid of the burden of emotions like envy, jealousy, and greed—because once we appreciate what we have, it no longer matters what others have. We then become more willing to help others and celebrate their joy with them, rather than putting them down or focusing on taking for ourselves in order to fill our sense of lack. The Mishnah in *Pirkei Avot* "איזה הוא עשיר השמח בחלקו" is usually translated as, "Who is rich? One who is happy with his lot," but it can also be explained as "one who is happy with *his* (i.e., the other person's) lot."

Upon arrival in Israel almost seven years later, I learned that in many ways gratitude is the essence of what it means to be Jewish. For a start, the Hebrew word for Jew is *Yehudi*, which comes from the word *l'hodot*, meaning to "thank, acknowledge, or admit." In other words, our very essence is to be grateful, to count our blessings and appreciate what we have. It is with this in mind that our Sages taught us to begin our day with "*Modeh ani*—I am grateful" as our first conscious thought. It is the beginning that holds the most potential, so starting the day with a (conscious) declaration of gratitude is really the best way to avoid getting out of bed on the wrong side.

> *There is a famous story of two men who went to visit Rav Zusha of Anipoli, who was famed for being a great tzaddik and master. He was extremely poor, living in a rundown shack and surviving on the bare minimum, often without enough food to feed his family. They arrived at his door and were shocked that the stories were true. His shelves were empty and he was wearing worn-out rags. They asked him, "How can you say the daily blessing, 'Blessed are you, Lord, our G-d, Who has given me everything I need?'" Rav Zusha calmly looked around, broke into a wide grin, and replied, "This must be all I need!"*

In the Creation narrative at the beginning of the Torah, we learn that although the trees and vegetation were created and placed in the earth on the third day, this was only in potential. It was only once Adam was created, and he recognized the goodness of rain and prayed for it, that the world came to life.[2]

From this we see that one of the foundational roles and attitudes of man in this world is *hakarat ha'tov*, recognizing the good in our lives. This doesn't just make us happier people. On a higher level, this attitude forms the basis of what our Sages teach is the purpose of Creation: to build a deep connection to the Source of good in our lives. In fact, Rav Itamar Schwartz learns from the *pasuk* in *Bereishit* (2:18), "It's not good for man to be alone," that the word "*tov*" actually means "connection," rendering *hakarat ha'tov*

---

2 See Rashi, *Bereishit* 2:5 from *Chulin* 60b:
מה טעם לא המטיר, לפי שאדם אין לעבוד את האדמה ואין מכיר בטובתם של גשמים, וכשבא אדם וידע שהם צורך לעולם התפלל עליהם וירדו, וצמחו האילנות והדשאים.

as "recognizing the connection."[3] We also come across this idea at the beginning of *Mesilat Yesharim*, which shares the verse from *Tehillim*, "ואני קרבת אלוקים לי טוב—Only closeness/connection to Hashem is called good."[4] By appreciating all the positive things in our lives and recognizing where they come from, we can create an authentic relationship with the Creator.

When I speak to groups, I often ask people to raise their hand if they want to be happy. Of course, everyone does. Then I ask, "Who knows what happiness is and how to achieve it?" At this point, unfortunately, very few, if any, people raise their hands. If we haven't defined our goal and planned out how to attain it, we're very unlikely to reach it.

Judaism teaches that real *simchah* has nothing to do with the external world. *Simchah* is an attitude to life. We say that we must be *b'simchah*, which means we need to be in a certain state of mind. The Baal Shem Tov points out that the word בשמחה (*b'simchah*) has the same letters as מחשבה (*machshavah*), thought. If our thoughts are in the right order, we will have a positive outlook on life and be in a stable state of true happiness, not reliant on external circumstances (which are beyond our control) to make us feel happy. It is our attitude that defines our experience of reality. With this in mind, one of the key attitude shifts[5] is for us to go from focusing on what we lack to always finding the best in things, focusing on and being grateful for every little blessing we have in our lives.

> *I have written this not to teach people what they don't know, rather to remind them of what they already know very well. However, just as much as the ideas are well-known, so too the neglect of them is common and forgetfulness is great.*
>
> *Mesilat Yesharim*[6]

3 *Getting to Know Your Soul* (Bilvavi Books), p. 193.

4 *Mesilat Yesharim*, chap. 1.

5 We will be looking at several others over the course of this book.

6 From the Introduction to *Mesilat Yesharim*:
החיבור הזה לא חברתיו ללמד לבני האדם את אשר לא ידעו, אלא להזכירם את הידוע להם כבר ומפורסם אצלם פירסום גדול אלא שכפי רוב פרסומם וכנגד מה שאמתתם גלויה לכל, כך ההעלם מהם מצוי מאד והשכחה רבה...

Many people know the advantages of living with gratitude, could probably teach a class on it, and even tell a couple of cool Chassidic stories to back up their point. But if after the class they get upset when they don't get the food they wanted, the ideas mean nothing. As with everything in life (and all the ideas in this book), it's not just enough to know and understand them. Ideas alone are almost useless.

Real transformation only comes from daily practice, discipline, and integration of the knowledge, turning it into applied wisdom. How many of us actually take the time to do the *avodah*—the real work to implement and live with these ideas? How often do we read books like this and skip the exercise part or comment on what a good exercise that would be, but never get around to doing it?

Real transformation only comes from daily practice, discipline, and integration of the knowledge, turning it into applied wisdom

It's not enough to only appreciate our legs when they hurt or when we see someone in a wheelchair. There has to be a conscious appreciation of our blessings several times throughout the day in order to ensure the promise of happiness this idea brings. That means not just recognizing and even listing what we are grateful for but taking time to actually *feel* a deep sense of gratitude.

With this in mind, here are a few tips for Enlightened Jewish Master gratitude training.

- **Recognize the good.** Choose one thing a day you have started to take for granted, e.g., your fridge, your legs, the guy who sweeps your street. Sit up straight, away from your phone, breathe deeply, and take three minutes to focus on *and feel* what a great blessing it is. If you need to, imagine what life would be like without it and use the relief you feel as the catalyst for gratitude. Then, take that feeling of gratitude and direct it toward Hashem, the Source of All Blessings. Articulate your gratitude in words.
- **Recognize the negative.** Notice when your mind is sending you negative, ungrateful thoughts such as, "If only I had

more..." "Not this for lunch again!" "Why did she deserve...and I didn't?" Smile gently at your *yetzer hara* and say, "I hear that, but at least I have..."

- **When expressing appreciation**, the more details the better. Details help you appreciate more and make the other person feel more appreciated. Swap "Thank you for dinner" with "Thank you for dinner. I can see how much effort you put in, and the chicken was particularly good."
- **Don't forget** to thank people for the things they are "meant to do." It's easy to thank people for the big things and overlook the day-to-day things they do for you that probably take more effort. It's easy to say thank you for a gift or a great meal, but what about the laundry and the dishes, the hard work to bring in money, or picking the kids up from school?
- **Write a list.** The golden oldie, this one is very important but usually stops being meaningful as people just write something down to fulfill the task. It is only effective if you take time to not only write down what you appreciate but to consciously feel your gratitude. To make it easier, have subtitles: my family, my health, my home, my job, etc. Once in a while, pull out the list and choose one thing to focus on, or just reflect on how many great things you have in your life.

Nice ideas? Great. Now actually make the time to do them! Don't live an "I should have" life.

Working in the orphanage in Kegalle woke me up very powerfully to this truth. The kids there appreciated their small blessings more than many of us appreciate our big ones. Seeing these kids and how little it took to deeply affect their lives helped me realize how much I have and therefore how much I have to give.

Seeing these kids and how little it took to deeply affect their lives helped me realize how much I have and therefore how much I have to give.

After two weeks in Kegalle, I felt I needed go somewhere totally on my own, even more remote, far from any civilization as I knew it. The option came up for me to go to the Sanasa branch in Monaragala, fifteen hours by bus southeast of Kegalle. Monaragala was the sort of place that would make even Sri Lankans wonder what on earth I was doing there. Once, on a bus ride between Kandy and Badulla (the closest town to Monaragala), in pouring rain on typically treacherous Sri Lankan roads, on a bus with maybe half its windows intact and no windscreen, I was chatting to a teacher from Colombo. We were all squeezed in as far into the middle of the bus as possible, trying hopelessly to avoid getting wet, praying that this journey, at breakneck speed along dangerous mountain roads (with a driver who constantly had to wipe the water off his face) would not end in disaster. When I replied, "Monaragala" to his question as to where I was going, he burst out laughing and said, "*Suddhu mali* (white brother), you are crazier than you look!"

I spent the days teaching English, washing my clothes on a rock and meditating in the local temple, where I would go each day for early morning and late afternoon prayers. I soon learned all the words to the chants and could join in with the monks in their sunrise and sunset services. I became very friendly with Rohan, the Sanasa caretaker, and his family and used to sit in the kitchen with them, helping peel the potatoes and carrying the huge cauldron of boiling rice from the fire to the dining room, laughing and joking as we tried to communicate in broken English and Sinhala. I didn't really realize what a stir I was causing by breaking the class boundaries in my ignorance of the caste system, which put the white English teacher far above the kitchen workers who were his best friends and closest confidants. It was one of the best times of my life, very simple and pure, unlike anything I had ever experienced. I was totally on my own, learning and growing; meditating, exercising and reading; interacting with genuine and friendly people in what was for me at the time, the most random place in the world. I was truly in my element.

Toward the end of my time there, Senerat decided to take all the English volunteers to his brother's village for a taste of even more rural Sri Lankan life.

We met in Kandy, and after a train journey, a bus ride sitting on the roof, and an hour hike through the countryside, we arrived in the "village," which actually turned out to be just one hut in the middle of a field. We were greeted warmly by the family, white teeth shining out through their wide and genuine smiles. The field was covered in small white round-headed flowers, I think chamomile, which Senerat's six-year-old niece ran out to collect. Five minutes later, the pot was boiling over the fire, and we all enjoyed a cup of some of the most interesting tea I've ever tasted. After talking to the family, with Senerat acting as translator, we met up with an old man and a few younger guys from a nearby village and went for a hike up into the mountains that surrounded the lake on all sides. As we scrambled over the final rocks to reach the plateau, we were met by a truly mind-quieting sight. The deep-orange sun was setting behind the vast plains, and I was suddenly hit by a transcendent feeling of awe at the vastness and beauty of Creation. It was a moment of epiphany, leaving me with the realization that I am just a small part of a much greater whole, that there is so much more to life than I could ever have imagined. I became aware that there is so much beauty, so much to achieve, so much beyond me and my personal needs—so much beyond the grind of the "real world" I had left behind. It made me feel small and humble, and yet at the same time more connected and empowered than I had ever felt before.

It made me feel small and humble, and yet at the same time more connected and empowered than I had ever felt before.

We made it down after dark and found a suitable place to camp for the night. While the others were having a rest, the village guys invited me to go fishing with them in the lake. The sun had already set and there was no light pollution (or electricity at all) in the area to dull the brilliant glow of the myriad stars illuminating the scene around us. Just before entering the lake, they gave me my weapons: a dull flashlight and a large knife. As I waded through the murky water, straining to catch sight of a fish, I took the opportunity to "zoom out" of my life and to locate myself in the world, as if looking down from space, getting a new perspective on the present moment and the absolute absurdity of what I was doing. The current scene was particularly random: a nice Jewish boy from North London standing knee-deep in the middle of a lake in central Sri Lanka, flashlight and spear at the ready, hoping to catch dinner. I didn't see a fish, let alone catch one, but the others were more successful and managed to provide the group with plenty to eat for dinner. (I sometimes wonder if they were just having fun with me, and had really bought the fish in the market earlier that day!) We got back to the campsite, where Senerat's sister-in-law started preparing the fish curry and rice for dinner. While the others sat in a circle around the fire, chopping vegetables, drinking beer, and sharing stories, Senerat told me to go with the old man to his village to collect some mats to sleep on. The man, with a strong smell of whiskey on his breath, had a rickety motorbike, which didn't look as though it would actually start up, let alone carry us both. As I got on the back of the bike, Senerat came over to me and whispered, "Take this with you, brother," as he pressed a big knife into my hand. Before I had time to protest, I was whisked off on a crazy fifty-kilometer-per-hour motorbike ride through the pitch-black Sri Lankan night, no roads or even dirt paths to be seen, drunken old man for a driver, having just been secretly slipped a large knife, presumably for protection should I need it. Twenty minutes later, we somehow arrived at a village of ten or so huts, and the man told me to wait on the bike while he collected the mats. I sat there clutching the knife, looking around me, waiting to be attacked from all sides. It occurred to me that even if I did manage to defend myself somehow, I was totally lost in the middle of nowhere, prey to the elements and whatever dangers were lurking in the Sri Lankan wilderness. Ten tense minutes later, the old man returned with twelve straw mats, and we made our way back to the campsite, fifty kilometers per hour again, but now with the added hazard of hanging on to the mats on my lap with one hand and the driver with the other. When we got back, we were greeted by the mouthwatering smell of freshly cooked fish curry, a large campfire, and some beers cooled off in the lake. Senerat came up to relieve me of the mats.

"Um...*aya*," I addressed him like always as "brother."

"Yes, brother?"

"Why did you give me the knife?"

"Oh, no problem, brother. I've just never met that man before, and there are dangerous people in these villages. He could have tried to harm you."

"Thanks, *aya*, very thoughtful of you," I said, resting my hand on his shoulder. At least he had the courtesy to give me a knife when he sent me off into the wilderness on a rickety old motorbike with an unknown, drunk, and possibly dangerous local villager.

After eating my fill, I lay down on my mat, looked up at the stars, and felt truly grateful that I was alive, well, and well-fed as I fell asleep to the sweet sound of the traditional Sri Lankan folk songs that pierced the starry night sky and echoed off the mountains all around.

CHAPTER 3

Thailand

The Philosopher and the Monk

It's 4:00 a.m.

I'm roused out of my uncomfortable sleep on the wooden bed with the wooden "pillow," in a room barely big enough for the bed and my bag, by the incessant ring of the bell. No, it's not Thai prison, it's Wat Suan Mokkh ten-day silent-meditation retreat in Surat Thani Province, Southern Thailand. I'm here with about fifty other foreigners all seeking peace of mind, mastery of thought, a quenching of desire: nibbana[1]*—enlightenment. I emerge from under my mosquito net and make my way outside, where I can hear splashing as the other half-asleep participants have already begun pouring buckets of cold water over themselves from the huge cement troughs in the courtyard. I join in the ritual—nothing like a cold bucket shower to wake you up in the morning. We trudge toward the meditation hall as the first grayish light begins to reveal the silhouettes of the palm trees lining the surrounding hills. Fifteen hours later we fall back into our wooden beds, another day of conscious breathing, conscious walking, conscious eating, consciously coming*

1 In the Pali language, used in Buddha's time. More commonly known in the West by its Sanskrit word, *nirvana*.

face-to-face with ourselves in a very real way. Away from any distractions—no TV, no phone, no reading, no writing, no computers, and only one meal a day—just us and our thoughts. We are learning to focus all our attention on our breath, trying to discover the inner peace, bliss, and higher awareness that lies underneath the constant babbling of the monkey mind.[2]

I arrived in Thailand toward the end of December 2000 and moved straight into my new home, the small village of Nong Pau Tan. Situated in the middle of the paddy and pineapple fields, two hundred kilometers south of Bangkok, Nong Pau Tan lies in the thinnest part of the country, nestled between the mountainous Kaeng Krachan National Park and the pristine coast of the Gulf of Thailand. The old wooden houses, badly paved roads, and population of simple farmers belied the large TVs and computer game consoles that could be found in many of the houses. It became clear that some form of digital entertainment to unwind after a hard day's work, whether in the office or the paddy fields, has become a top priority throughout the world, no matter what the situation and standard of living.

My host was Kru Salee, a forty-five-year-old schoolteacher who had been a student of mine in my English teacher-training course in London. We hit it off immediately, and she invited me to stay with her family and come teach in the village school. As my time in Sri Lanka was drawing to an end, I took her up on the offer and so started my one-and-a-half-year sojourn in the "Land of Smiles."[3]

The first couple of weeks, as was the case in most of the countries in which I lived, were pretty lonely and challenging. Being the only *farang* (foreigner), looking so different from everyone else, unable to communicate or understand what anyone was saying about me, was very disempowering and humbling. Salee introduced me to the boys in the village, and once again, as happened so many times throughout

2 A term referring to the nature of the mind, which is always unsettled and jumping around, often causing trouble.

3 Popular nickname for Thailand.

my travels, the saving grace came in the form of the good ol' universal language—football.[4] Bring a group of boys together, give them a ball, and they'll be best friends, or worst enemies, within half an hour.

Every day after school and work, all the guys in the village would gather at the football pitch, pick teams, and slog it out for the next two hours. After the game, we would get a bottle of cheap Thai whiskey and some cold beers, and tuck into some local delicacies such as *som tam* (spicy papaya salad) or *kuay teow* (noodle soup). Once in a while, someone would grab a duck that was innocently waddling around, twist its neck, and throw it into the bushes until it stopped struggling. They'd pull off the feathers, boil it up with some spices and vegetables, and within half an hour everyone would be relishing a fine duck soup to go with the whiskey and beer. After volunteering in the village school for a few weeks, I got a job teaching English in a university about a forty-minute drive up the road toward Bangkok, and between my football buddies, university students and Kru Salee, I was speaking highly conversational Thai within three months.

Socially settled, financially stable, and now able to communicate, it was time to go in search of the master and the practice that was the motivating factor for my travels in the first place. I found him in the form of Tan Medhi, a forty-year-old Thai man who had renounced his life as a lawyer in Bangkok and was now living the ascetic life (replete with shaved head and orange robes) of a monk in the forest temple that became my second home in Thailand. I would join him on his early-morning alms round on which he would collect his simple food for the day from the nearby villages, and we'd discuss life, meaning, meditation, and philosophy for hours. Then we would find our own spot by the pond, where we'd settle into our meditation practice, lulled into a peaceful state of mind by the chirping of the cicadas and the croaking of the frogs. We always joked that this would make a good photo for the cover of our first

4 Soccer.

book—*The Philosopher and the Monk*. After my initial efforts back in my Sri Lankan temple, my real quest for mastering the "monkey mind" had truly begun.

> *You are what you think. All that you are arises from your thoughts. With your thoughts you make your world.*
>
> *Thai saying*

> *It is important that you do not neglect taking care of guarding your thoughts...for the majority of imperfection and rectification of one's action is only through them.*
>
> *Chovot HaLevavot*[5]

In the East, originating in the Chinese and Japanese Buddhist traditions, the mind is often referred to as "monkey mind"—constantly jumping around, rarely still and at rest. From the second we wake up until the second we fall asleep we have a constant companion, commenting, judging, comparing, doubting, worrying, regretting, and generally causing all sorts of mischief. The mind takes over, and rather than us controlling it and using it when we need, it runs wild, often to negative places.

Try to stop thinking for ten seconds and just focus on your breath and you'll see that it's almost impossible. How many times have you lain in bed, wanting to sleep but unable to because your mind was in overdrive? If you had a friend who spoke to you the way you often speak to yourself, how long would you let them remain your friend? How many times have you gone over the same train of thought, whether rehearsing a speech to give a person who hurt you (which more often than not never takes place), replaying a mistake you made, or worrying about whether you remembered to turn off the oven or lock the door?

The mind is the backdrop to everything we feel and do, ultimately creating our whole experience of reality—for good or for bad. Most of

5 Chap. 6.

us are controlled by external circumstances—if we miss the bus, we get frustrated; if someone compliments us, we feel great; if it's raining, we're down; if it's sunny, everything is good in the world. The external world acts as a stimulus, which is filtered through our beliefs, creates thoughts, and those thoughts give rise to emotions.

Let's do a thought experiment to demonstrate this.

You go to the bank and get in line, and someone pushes in front of you. How does it make you feel? How do you react?

The truth is that it depends on many factors:

- **What you believe and how you feel about yourself.** If you have low self-esteem, you think, "I can't believe I let someone do that again," or "I deserved that," and then you'd feel bad about yourself and perhaps cry or withdraw to your room. Yet if you are arrogant,[6] you may think, "How dare they? Do they know who I am?" and you'd feel anger and start shouting.
- **What you think of the other person.** If you notice it was a close friend you haven't seen for a while, you'll react very differently than if it were someone you don't know or don't like.
- **Your mood.** If you just had a big argument with your boss and stormed out, you may make a fuss, whereas if you just won the lottery, you may just let it go.

What this demonstrates is that it is not actually the external circumstances that dictate our experience of reality, it is any number of internal factors and beliefs.

In Judaism, our unhealthy drives and destructive mind patterns are referred to as the *yetzer hara*, the inclination toward negativity. This prevents us from moving toward achieving great things, and guides us toward doing, thinking, feeling, and saying things that are harmful to us and those around us.

It is surprising then that the Midrash teaches that the *yetzer hara* is our best friend.[7] How can this be? It's because only by overcoming,

---

6 Which usually comes as a cover-up for low self-esteem.

7 *Bereishit Rabbah* 9:7.

conquering, taming, and ultimately redirecting its energy that we become true masters. This is expressed in what is (for me) one of the most essential teachings in *Pirkei Avot*:

איזהו גיבור?

Who is the strong one?

הכובש את יצרו.

The one who conquers his own inclination toward negativity.[8]

The real *gibor*, or master, is the one who has learned to tame the monkey mind, to quiet the chatter, and retain awareness of the positive, steering away from giving room for the *yetzer hara* to lead the way. This is incredibly empowering, as it means it is really up to us. We often can't control what happens, but if we are conscious enough, we can certainly control how we let it affect us.

We often can't control what happens, but if we are conscious enough, we can certainly control how we let it affect us.

My daughter, Tamara Menucha, who was three at the time, learned this lesson in a very powerful way. One Shabbat we were sitting together reading a book and she asked me for some ice cream. I went to the freezer and was faced with a terrible situation—no ice cream! I returned to Nucha, as she likes to be called, and informed her of the situation, to which she quite understandably reacted by starting to whine. Now, although it is important to learn to control our thoughts, *feelings* need to be dealt with in a different way; they need to be acknowledged and accepted. Sometimes when we feel upset or jealous about something, we beat ourselves up saying, "I shouldn't feel upset," "I'm bad for feeling jealous." This doesn't help the situation at all—not only do we feel upset, we then make ourselves feel wrong for feeling that way, which makes us feel even worse! We need to learn to accept our feelings and just experience them, giving them space to manifest and express in a healthy way, and in this way they will pass more quickly. In fact, Rashi

8 *Pirkei Avot* 4:1.

comments that all difficult things in life are because "our consciousness is not wide enough to accept them and we don't have room in our heart just to feel the pain."[9] Only once we do this can we work on controlling the thoughts that would otherwise perpetuate the negative feeling.

I therefore tried to validate Nucha's feelings, telling her I could hear how upset she was, that it was quite understandable, and that I was upset too because I also wanted ice cream. Nucha, not appeased, continued to whine. Now time for the lesson:

> *Abba: Nucha, I've got a question. Do you think whining will make more ice cream?*
>
> *(Nucha looks confused.)*
>
> *Abba: Look, I'm getting a bowl from the cupboard and we'll whine together and maybe we can make ice cream. (Abba gets bowl and brings it to the table.)*
>
> *Abba: "Aarrrhh, noooo, it's not fair…"*
>
> *(Nucha smiles. From whining to confusion to laughter—good progress.)*
>
> *Abba (seeing his chance): Nucha, I want to teach you an important lesson. We both want ice cream, but there is no ice cream, and we can't get any. So now we have a choice. We can choose to be upset by this for the rest of Shabbat, or choose to be okay with it. If we want to be sad, we can have these thoughts: "It's not fair, I want ice cream, I bet my friends have ice cream, I'll never have ice cream, I hate not having ice cream…," and if we want to be happy, we can have these thoughts: "I can have some cake instead, I can play with my toys, maybe I can have ice cream tomorrow, I'm happy for my friends that they have ice cream…" So really, we can choose how we feel. It's up to us!*
>
> *Nucha (after some thought): Okay, Abba, let's choose to be happy.*
>
> *(Nucha takes a cookie and we go back to reading the book.)*

---

9 *Bamidbar* 21:4: .אין דעתו רחבה לקבל אותו הדבר, ואין לו מקום בתוך לבו לגור שם אותו הצער

This was an awesome lesson for a three-year-old to understand, possibly the most important lesson she will ever learn. Whereas we often can't choose our circumstances and control the world around us, we can start raising our consciousness and choosing how to relate to what goes on and how we feel about it.[10]

All of us will face pain and challenges in our lives, both physical and emotional. Our job is to be conscious and disciplined enough to be able to acknowledge and express our feelings in a healthy way, and then guide our thoughts to process them and move on in a positive way. All challenges in life are tests in order to push us to grow; the bigger the challenge, the greater the opportunity to become a *tzaddik*. We can be a victim of our circumstances, or use them to grow and connect.[11] In this way, we take full responsibility for writing our own life stories—not giving the power of our happiness over to things that are out of our control.

We take full responsibility for writing our own life stories—not giving the power of our happiness over to things that are out of our control.

In this vein, our Sages urge us to develop *hishtavut*, השתוות—equanimity. Equanimity means not letting the external world dictate how we feel. As the *Chovot HaLevavot* teaches:

---

10 I'm not, G-d forbid, belittling anyone's suffering and suggesting they just change their perspective so easily. It's hard enough to control the mind and choose to be positive even when the painful situations aren't so challenging—such as not getting ice cream, being caught in a traffic jam, or stubbing a toe. It takes great effort in reprogramming and training the mind. How much more so for people faced with real trauma, abuse, clinical depression, or chemical imbalances. In these cases, the one to blame is the person or condition inflicting the pain, not the victim. The more severe the pain, the harder it is to relate to it in a positive way. It could take years of therapy, healing, and/or medication to overcome these challenges. In the end, though, the healing will always come when the energy has been released and the mind has come to terms with the pain and can see it in a more positive way, for instance, by turning the pain into purpose, such as by helping others going through the same thing.

11 This doesn't mean we won't feel pain. When someone dies we don't just say, "This too is for the best" and carry on as normal. We sit and mourn for seven days. Even though we know it's for the best, it doesn't mean it's not sad and painful. It's just that the pain doesn't turn into uncontrollable suffering.

> *A pious one asked his friend, "Have you reached equanimity?"*
>
> *[The friend] asked, "In what matter?"*
>
> *[The pious one] said, "Is it equal in your eyes if you are praised or insulted?"*
>
> *[The friend] said, "No."*
>
> *[The pious one] said, "Then you have not yet arrived. Put in the effort and maybe you'll arrive, for it is the greatest level and the most precious virtue."*[12]

For many people, their mood and sense of self are controlled by external factors beyond their control. Praise and insult, successes and failures should all be taken as ways to introspect and grow rather than cause arrogance on the one hand, or low self-esteem on the other.[13] How do we achieve this state? The Baal Shem Tov taught that the well-known phrase "שויתי ה' לנגדי תמיד" (often translated as "I place Hashem before me at all times") can also be read as "שויתי—I have equanimity"! Why? Because "ה' לנגדי תמיד—everything is coming from Hashem" and is exactly what I need for my personal growth.[14] Once we integrate the fact that everything that happens to us is for the best, we can start seeing things as a test, given to us in order to lift us up[15] to higher levels of personal mastery and G-d-consciousness.

Praise and insult, successes and failures should all be taken as ways to introspect and grow rather than cause arrogance on the one hand, or low self-esteem on the other.

12 *Chovot HaLevavot* 5:5
כבר אמרו על אחר מן החסידים שאמר לחבירו הנשתוית אמר לו באיזה ענין אמר לו נשתוה בעיניך השבח והגנות א"ל לא א"ל א"כ עדיין לא הגעת השתדל אולי תגיע אל המדרגה הזאת כי היא העליונה שבמדרגות החסידים ותכלית החמודות

13 Equanimity does not mean emotional detachment or stoicism; it means emotional intelligence. In fact, someone with healthy equanimity can be even more involved, caring, and available for others.

14 *Tzivat HaRivash, siman* 2.

15 The root of the Hebrew word for test, *nisayon*, means to lift up.

In order to attain these levels, some sort of meditation practice is essential. The primary aim of meditation is to tame the mind, to stop it jumping around so fast and uncontrollably, to observe it, focus it, calm it down, and taste the stillness hiding beneath. The first thing one notices when starting to meditate is that we are hardly in control of what goes on in our heads.

There are, in general, two types of meditation:

Passive meditation is the exercise of either focusing your entire awareness on one thing—such as your breath or a sound or anything that brings you fully into the present moment—helping you move away from the hectic, fast-moving, uncontrolled thought processes, or just observing all thoughts, sensations, and feelings that arise, without judging or getting caught up in them. After a while, the breaks in between the thoughts get longer as the focus gets more consistent and effortless, at which point it feels like the deep peace you experience when the baby finally stops screaming and drops off to sleep at three o'clock in the morning. We've all experienced this sublime state naturally for a few moments, perhaps when listening to classical music or the birds singing in the park or when we feel the sun on our face on a beautiful spring day. Life is often like treading water, with constant waves of challenges, emotions, and responsibilities rolling toward us. So much of our energy is taken up with thinking that on the rare occasions that we rise above our thoughts (even for a short while), it is like withdrawing onto the beach, finally resting, finding serenity, and recharging. Meditation helps us find the space to be more aware of what's going on in our minds, without drowning in our thoughts. It's amazing to realize that serenity isn't something we need to strive for at some point in the future. When the mind is clear and calm, we experience the real peace and tranquility that is always there, waiting to be revealed.

Active meditation involves using the mind in a focused and controlled way to get a deeper understanding into things, create certain thoughts, feelings and beliefs, and approach life in a more positive and empowered way.

An example of this in Jewish teachings is *hitbonenut*, contemplation. Rambam teaches us to use this technique to build *ahavat Hashem*, love of G-d.

> *When a person contemplates His wondrous and great deeds and creations and appreciates His infinite wisdom that surpasses all comparison, he will immediately love, praise, and glorify Him, yearning with tremendous desire to know the Great Name.*[16]

It was a great surprise and pleasure for me to find that Judaism has a rich and deep tradition of meditation and spiritual practices for increased awareness and self-mastery. This is not only in Kabbalistic literature. The Talmud[17] teaches that the early pious masters would take an hour before praying just to prepare for what they were about to do The Rambam says they used that hour "להשקיט מחשבתם—to quiet their thoughts," a classic example of passive meditation before stepping into the active meditation that is Jewish prayer.[18]

The idea of *kavanah*—how we direct our thoughts and attention while praying, doing mitzvot, and in life in general—is of such huge importance in halachic, Talmudic, and Chassidic writings that the *Shulchan Aruch*[19] rules according to the Rishonim,[20] who hold that "מצות צריכות כוונה—a mitzvah does not count unless it is done with the right focus and intention."[21]

Judaism teaches that we are not our thoughts, especially not the critical, judgmental, negative ones. Essentially, we are the pure

---

16 *Hilchot Yesodei HaTorah* 2:2:
בשעה שיתבונן האדם במעשיו וברואיו הנפלאים הגדולים ויראה מהן חכמתו שאין לה ערך ולא קץ מיד הוא אוהב ומשבח ומפאר ומתאוה תאוה גדולה לידע השם הגדול.

17 *Berachot* 30b.

18 Rebbe Elimelech of Lizhensk writes in his seminal work, *Noam Elimelech*, that in that hour before prayer they would sit to contemplate and be astonished at the greatness of G-d (the word *shohin*, to sit, shares a root with the word *mista'ah*, to be astonished), a classic form of active meditation (see *Parashat Bo*, first piece). Ramchal, in *Mesilat Yesharim*, teaches that they would do both, divesting themselves of any foreign thoughts and filling themselves with *yirah* and *ahavat Hashem* (chap. 17, "*K'niyat HaTaharah*").

19 *Orach Chaim* 60:6, 589:8.

20 Torah Sages who lived from the eleventh to fifteenth century.

21 This could be a whole book in itself. In brief, there are two levels of *kavanah* for mitzvot: the first is simply the awareness that you are doing the action for the sake of doing a mitzvah, while the second, higher level is doing it with consciousness, presence, and true sincerity of heart.

consciousness/soul that lies beyond the mind, and we can watch, conquer, control, and use it. Furthermore, developing this level of consciousness is not just "a nice thing to do" if we want to. Just like we are not allowed to put pig in our mouths, there are certain thoughts that we are not allowed to entertain in our consciousness because they disconnect us from our pure spiritual essence. Just like we have to establish a warm, loving home, we have to cultivate positive and pure thoughts in our minds. This means that part of following the Torah's guidelines for living our best lives entails becoming people who can consciously observe our thoughts and emotions as they arise and start to interact with them from a place of *mochin d'gadlut*—expanded awareness. Rather than identifying with our thoughts, getting caught up in them, and reacting to them in speech, feeling, and action, it means viewing them from a higher perspective, where we make the active choice of which thoughts we allow to go through our minds. In a sense, this is what it really means to be an observant Jew: having the ability to observe thoughts and emotions without being defined or controlled by them.

Just like we have to establish a warm, loving home, we have to cultivate positive and pure thoughts in our minds.

> *A man came to the Kotzker Rebbe and told him that when he davens, he has all sorts of thoughts. The Kotzker Rebbe told him there was nothing he could do for him. The man left, a little dejected, and returned to his village. On arriving home, he saw some men walking in and out of his house, taking his furniture out and leaving it on the sidewalk. The chassid was irate! "What are you doing? You can't just walk into someone's house without permission!" The men apologized and told him that they were just following orders. The Kotzker Rebbe had instructed them to do it. The chassid stormed back to the Rebbe and started shouting, "Not only did you not help me, but then you get people to come and take things out of my house!" The Rebbe inquired as to why he was so upset about it. "Because it's my house, and no one can enter my house without permission!"*

> *The Rebbe smiled. "This is your house too," he said, pointing at the chassid's head. "No thoughts can come in without your permission."*

So how do we start implementing this practically in our lives? Can we learn basic meditation techniques without leaving home for a ten-day silent retreat or sitting crossed-legged in a cave somewhere? Can we start to consciously choose what thoughts we allow to come in to our heads?

Try out these Enlightened Jewish Master meditation and mind-control training tips.

- **Basic meditation technique.** Make sure you're in a quiet place with no distractions; your phone should be far away. Sit comfortably on the floor or a chair, as long as your back is straight. (Lying down is not a good idea; you'll fall asleep!) Set an alarm for five minutes. Breathe deeply and steadily in through your nose, out through your mouth. Concentrate on your breath going in and out. If you are normal, you will be able to do this for about half a second before your mind starts wandering—thinking, planning, judging—and you start having feelings such as boredom, frustration, and so on. As soon as you notice your mind all over the place—smile! Feel good about yourself for catching it and gently bring it back to focusing on the breath coming in and going out. Repeat the exercise. Notice that the time spent being able to focus on the breath increases and the wander time gets shorter. Notice the feeling of peace that starts to arise as you have a break from incessant thinking.
- **Feeling emotions.** When we feel an emotion—loneliness, pain, sadness, anger—we often think about it and then judge both the emotion and ourselves: *Why am I lonely? It's not fair that I'm lonely. Other people aren't lonely. If I was married, I wouldn't be lonely. I hate being lonely. I shouldn't complain*

about feeling lonely, I should be more grateful... Ultimately, the thoughts don't help. They just perpetuate the emotion and stop you from experiencing and feeling it. Try to just breathe and feel the emotion without thinking about it. Breathe in and say, "I feel really lonely now...and that's okay." Do this until you have really felt the feeling and see how, having been experienced, the feeling starts to clear up.

- **Write a list** of negative thoughts and beliefs, regrets and pains that often come to mind, serve no positive purpose, and make you feel bad, such as, "If only..." "I'm so stupid..." "I'll never get married..." During the day, when one of these arises, rather than entertaining it, judging it, fighting it, giving in to it, or continuing it, just acknowledge it, smile, and gently say, "Hi, thanks for coming, but you can't control me anymore." Replace it with a positive thought.[22] *Your experience of reality is dictated by which thoughts you make significant.* Choose not to give significance to negative thoughts (which come from the *yetzer hara*), and apply what Shlomo HaMelech said, "גם זה יעבור—this (thought) too shall pass."
- **Equanimity/*emunah* training.** Start implementing the knowledge that everything we see, hear, and experience is coming from Hashem. Before getting upset, remind yourself that the guy davening too loudly next to you, the missed bus, broken glasses, the bill you can't pay—they are all just challenges to help us grow.[23] Start saying, "*Gam zu l'tovah*—This too is for the best,"[24] even if you don't really feel it. After training yourself to say this all the time, you'll actually start to believe it.

---

22 Yes, I do know that it's easier said than done. Just try it—you'll get better. Check out my class on YouTube, "Judaism: Mastering the Mind," for a full explanation of this method.

23 That doesn't mean you have to remain passive. Hashem put them in your life so you could grow and to change them if you can. You can talk to the guy after davening, stand up against injustice you see, make sure you get to the bus stop earlier. It just means you skip the "getting angry and annoyed" part.

24 See *Taanit* 21a.

I sometimes wonder what Tan Medhi[25] would think if he could see me from his place next to the peaceful pond in Suan Mokkh, at that moment fifteen minutes before Shabbat candle lighting on Friday afternoon, when the kids are crying, the guests are arriving, I'm still not dressed, the floor needs to be cleaned, and then someone spills the red wine all over the white tablecloth. He may wonder why I gave up the serenity of temple life for the *balagan* of family life, with rent to pay and mouths to feed.

Then again, he may realize that it's one thing to control your thoughts and emotions while cut off from the challenges of relationships, responsibilities, and general everyday life, but quite another to overcome your ego while fully immersed in the world, where the test is far greater and therefore the mastery of the monkey mind has to be on the highest level imaginable.

It was a few days after my second ten-day silent retreat that I reached a state of "no-mind," of being totally in the present moment, the chatter of the monkey completely silenced, and all this totally unplanned and with absolutely no effort...for a few seconds at least.

I spent much of my free time in Thailand climbing through the jungle, swimming in reservoirs, scrambling along waterfalls, and hanging out on the beach. I was on one of my afternoon adventures in the forests that surrounded my village, on the way to the reservoir for a meditation session and afternoon swim. As I emerged through the undergrowth, ready to settle in, I was met by a loud noise that sounded like a very fat man snoring extremely loudly. I looked toward the source of the sound, feeling a bit annoyed that my plans of quiet solitude had been disturbed, and my heart and mind literally stopped for a few moments. About fifty feet away from me, raised up to its full height of around one and a half meters, looking me straight in the eye, was a huge snake, hood fully spread in attack mode, growling and hissing like a large dog, ready to deliver a deadly strike. I didn't know a snake could make such a sound. I was paralyzed with fear, and for

25 My monk friend in the temple in Thailand.

a few moments of ultimate presence, there were no thoughts at all in my consciousness. A few seconds later, my mind kicked back in as thoughts rushed through my head: *What if it's a spitting cobra that can accurately spit venom from up to thirty feet? What if they hunt in packs and its friends are coming up behind me?*

If I had been bitten there, I'd have been pretty much done for—in the middle of nowhere, no phone, no chance. For a while it was just a staring match; a helpless little Jew far from home against a pretty angry, deadly beast, very much at home. Needless to say, it was me who backed off first, walking slowly away, eyes always on my enemy, intensely alert and pitifully afraid. After regaining some composure, I decided I had to get some identifying marks, because if I'd get out of this alive, I'd need to describe the snake to my best friend, Ben, who knows all about nature, so he could identify it. I took two careful steps forward, possibly a bad move given the situation, and noted the round markings on either side of its throat. I then turned and ran as fast as I could through the undergrowth, jumped on my scooter, and sped away from the reservoir, never to return.

I sat on my porch that evening, pondering the fact that it takes many, many hours of meditation practice to come to the state of no-mind, yet when faced with exhilarating near-death experiences, we get there instantly and with no effort. This is why so many people do bungee jumping and skydiving (and even drugs), or just distract themselves through TV and social media, in an effort to become totally present, free for a while from the constant barrage of thoughts. The difference is that the ultimate presence forced upon us by external factors or the escape we find in entertainment, is short-lived and doesn't really transform us. The peace and presence that comes from meditation creates lasting insight and real change, bringing us to a higher state of awareness and enabling us take control of the monkey mind on an ongoing basis.

It was about time for evening services, so I made my way to the temple, where I took my spot among the monks and gently focused my mind on my breath, looking to tap into a place of no-mind, just this time for a more sustained period and without the fear of imminent death.

The next day, word came back from Ben. As I had suspected, I'd been face-to-face with one of the world's most deadly snakes—a king cobra.

CHAPTER 4

Laos

Being the Go-Between

One of my favorite books growing up was Kim, by Rudyard Kipling. It's about a young English boy who was born and subsequently orphaned in British-ruled India. I was so enamored with the streetwise kid—running across rooftops, doing deals, and learning the ways of the world—who on the one hand was of European ancestry, yet on the other hand was equally, if not more, comfortable among the locals. I prided myself on being somewhat like him, living on the edge between locals and travelers, speaking both languages, knowing both cultures—the connector, not fully part of either world. I used to walk off into the mountains and find a village where I would stay for a few days, helping with the farming and household chores, taking part in village life, festivals, and ceremonies, learning local folk songs, and truly experiencing the land. Then I'd hit the traveler hot spots to check out the scene before retreating back into the hills.

Nowhere more did I take on this role than in Laos, not so much by choice, but rather because I erred in thinking that my Thai bank card would work there. That left me with forty dollars in cash to get me through Laos for a month, which wasn't impossible if I stayed in a village somewhere, but would certainly not allow *me to travel around visiting all the places and taking part in all the activities I had planned to. As I withdrew my bank card from the ATM machine on the Laos side of the border, having had my request for money denied, I felt the spirit of Kim awakening inside me, and I relished the idea of relying on my wits and experience to get me through the next month in a new country, with unforeseeable challenges and adventures awaiting around every corner. By the end of my excursion, I could certainly confirm for myself Rudyard Kipling's wise words in Kim: "This is a brief life, but in its brevity it offers us some splendid moments, some truly meaningful adventures."*

I arrived in Luang Prabang, Laos, on May 7, 2002, having taken the two-day, slow boat ride down the Mekong River from the northern Thai border. The Mekong winds its majestic way from its source in the Tibetan Plateau through China, Burma, Thailand, Laos, Cambodia, and Vietnam before emptying out 4,350 kilometers later into the South China Sea. All along her banks, which are framed by mountains and jagged rocks, families go about their daily lives, which center almost totally around the river: washing themselves, fishing, playing, doing laundry, collecting water for cooking, as well using it to move around between villages for bartering purposes. It was not uncommon to see six-year-olds carrying their two-year-old siblings on their backs, filthy and in rags but with huge smiles, sparkling eyes, and the joy of childhood freedom shining on their faces. Once again, I became acutely aware of the fact that many poor people in the third world seemed to be more content than many wealthy people in the "developed" world, with all its privileges.

The language in Laos is very similar to Thai, just a few subtle changes and nuances that I picked up on the boat ride. As had become my tradition, I learned a couple of local folk songs as soon as I could, seeing as this was the best way to get a deeper insight into their lives and culture, endear myself to the locals, and open up a more intimate and authentic relationship with them, helping me be accepted as "part of the tribe."

On disembarking, we were met with a truly enchanting scene. As the cultural capital of Laos and a UNESCO[1] heritage site, Luang Prabang is a vibrant city, a fusion of traditional Lao wooden houses, colorful Buddhist temples, and French colonial buildings from the eighteenth and nineteenth centuries, all surrounded by lush forested mountains, home to picturesque waterfalls and ancient caves.

My first stop was a family-owned guest house, where began my banter, "I'm not a real *farang*. I may have the body of a *farang*, but I have the heart of a Laos person!" (Cue the folk song, much to the delight of the family.) "I'm not a rich Western tourist. I live in a small village in Thailand, just a normal poor man. I'll help you out, what work do you need me to do?"

Eventually, the mother had an idea. Many Thai and Laotian boys become novice monks for a few weeks or months to gain merit for their family, as something to do in the school holidays, or because they have become orphaned or been abandoned by their family. They shave their heads, don the orange robes, and enter the temple, where they keep the Ten Precepts[2] and learn Buddhist philosophy, meditation, and some secular subjects. Often, they don't take it all that seriously, because for many of them, it's just a tradition they (resentfully) have to go through. The mother thought that maybe having a *farang* teacher who could speak English and Lao and was familiar with Buddhist concepts and practice would be what the boys needed to inspire them to make the most of their enforced monastic existence.

So that's how I became a *rebbi* for the novice Buddhist monks in one of the main temples in Luang Prabang! I taught them English, Buddhist philosophy, and meditation, and, boys being boys, showed them a thing or two with a football at break time. In the afternoons, I'd join the other

---

1 The United Nations Educational, Scientific, and Cultural Organization.

2 To refrain from destroying living creatures; to refrain from taking that which is not given; to refrain from immorality; to refrain from incorrect speech; to refrain from intoxicating drinks and drugs, which lead to carelessness; to refrain from eating at the forbidden time (i.e., after noon); to refrain from dancing, singing, music, entertainment; to refrain from wearing garlands, using perfumes, and beautifying the body with cosmetics; to refrain from lying on a high or luxurious sleeping place; to refrain from accepting gold and silver (money).

farang hanging out by the river, and toward sunset, I'd walk up into the hills to find some peace beyond the hustle and bustle of town life, then make my way "home" to the guesthouse to share dinner and stories with my new family. I soon found my routine, and once again, rather than being a tourist just visiting a place, I felt like I was really living there, having an authentic experience with the locals, and hopefully leaving a positive mark on all those whose paths I crossed.

After a week, I decided it was time to head for Vang Vieng, the main backpacker spot in Laos, boasting captivating untouched scenery, plenty of cafés and chill-out places, and the famous river-tubing tour, which involved driving to the drop-off point ten kilometers up the Nam Song River and floating all the way back down on a huge tractor tire. On the way, locals on the river banks would throw out ropes and pull you in to partake of local food, have a go on huge swings and zip lines from which you could catapult into the river, and consume a fair amount of alcohol and other intoxicating substances. Although you can still go tubing there, the crazy backpacker party was brought to a halt in 2012 when the Lao government was forced by international pressure to crack down on the riverside bars, as several travelers, unsurprisingly, didn't make it back to town alive.

It was in Vang Vieng that my inner Kim really came out as I played the go-between for the locals and transitory backpackers—who often made up over fifty percent of the otherwise sleepy town's population. The deal was that if I could get some *farang* to stay in their guesthouse, go tubing with their organization, or eat in their restaurant, I would be rewarded with all these things for free as my pay. So it really ended up as a "win-win-win" situation. The travelers got discounts on their rooms, activities, or food, the local owners got more business, and I got free room, board, tours, and adventure activities to boot.

However, still driven by the quest for self-mastery and enlightenment, every morning before sunrise, as the rest of the *farang* slept off their hangovers, and every evening before the café where I worked started filling up again, I'd make my way to the local temple to join the monks in their trance-inducing chanting. I would sink into the now-familiar feeling of inner calm, detached from the physical world with all its challenges, beyond body consciousness, going deeper and deeper into states of one-pointedness and no-mind, a little Jewish Buddha in the making...

> *Drop by drop the water bucket is filled. Likewise, the wise man, gathering it little by little, fills himself with good.*
>
> *Laos Proverb*

> *All Divine service depends on the fixing of character traits.*
>
> *Vilna Gaon, Even Sheleimah*

According to Buddhist tradition, Siddhartha Gautama (later referred to as the Buddha) was born in Lumbini, which is modern-day Nepal, around 2,560 years ago. He was a prince, living in luxury, until one day, on a walk outside the palace grounds, he came into contact with the reality of old age, sickness, and death. This set him off on his search to discover the meaning of life and to bring an end to the cycle of birth, suffering, death, and rebirth. A full look into Buddhist philosophy is far beyond the scope of this book, but in brief, the Buddha taught the path of overcoming *dukkha*, the un-satisfactoriness of life.

According to Buddhist philosophy, everything in existence is *anijja*, impermanent, and *shunyata*, empty of intrinsic existence and meaning. It is the fact that we get attached to things in this world, including our own ego, that causes us suffering. He taught that even our ego is an illusion and that really there is *anatta*, no underlying self, no individual eternal soul, and by extension of that, not necessarily an infinite Divine Being Who created and controls it all.[3] We suffer in life because we either crave things we don't have, or get upset when the things and relationships we do have come to an end. By realizing that really there

3 Buddha never spoke about the origin of life and creation because he believed we can't get the answer to those questions. There is debate as to whether he was an atheist or agnostic.

is no "me" and no "mine," we break the attachment to and craving for things of this world. If there is no "I," there can be no feeling of "I" am unhappy. Of course, the philosophy is much more complex and deep than I can do justice to in this one paragraph (not to mention the fact that there are different schools of Buddhism that teach slightly different things), but it will have to suffice as a general overview for now.

Although its core philosophy is very different to that of Judaism, not least of all because they don't believe in the soul or G-d (which are the foundational principles of Jewish belief), there are many insightful teachings and practices that the paths share. One of these is the fundamental importance of the development and perfection of character traits. Buddha identified the three core negative traits or defilements (*kilesa*) as *lobha*, *dosa*, and *moha*—greed, anger, and ignorance. From these spring all other negative traits, including jealousy, hatred, lust, doubt, arrogance, and so on. He also taught that opposite these defilements there are four main traits that must be cultivated: *metta*, *karuna*, *mudita*, and *uppekha*—loving-kindness, compassion, sympathetic joy, and equanimity. It is through the realization that there is no ego, no "me" and "mine," that one can wipe out the negative character traits and develop the positive ones, thereby attaining *nibbana*, enlightenment—an egoless, unattached state, leaving one free from the suffering that accompanies life. In fact, the word *nibbana* actually means "quenching," meaning to put out the flames of these passions and wrong notions.

Although the emphasis on these character traits is somewhat similar, the Jewish path to attaining this is almost diametrically opposed to the Buddhist one. Rather than saying there is no self and that by seeing beyond the ego we will relinquish anger and fear and develop love and compassion, the Jewish approach to character refinement is that by actually connecting to, identifying with, and manifesting our true self, our pure spiritual essence, we can manifest our Godly nature in the world. Every morning we say, "אלהי נשמה שנתת בי טהורה היא—My G-d, the soul You have given me is pure," and the prophet Yeshayahu[4] taught

4 *Yeshayahu* 60:21.

that "עמך כלם צדיקים—We are all fully righteous, enlightened beings." It doesn't say that we **will be** *tzaddikim*, but that we are already *tzaddikim*—right here and now.[5] The only issue is that we don't often think, feel, speak, or act like *tzaddikim*. Yet just like an elephant who dresses up like a chicken, makes chicken noises, acts like a chicken, and eats chicken food is still really an elephant, when we strip away the thoughts, speech, and actions that are not in line with our soul, we reveal our essential enlightened, connected, healthy, pure selves. So really, Judaism isn't a path to achieving enlightenment, it's a path to revealing that you are already enlightened.

Judaism isn't a path to achieving enlightenment, it's a path to revealing that you are already enlightened.

We see this idea in *Pirkei Avot*[6] in two Mishnayot, which seem on the surface puzzling.

The first Mishnah teaches that there are four types of people who donate to charity:

1. One who donates but doesn't want others to donate
2. One who doesn't donate but wants others to donate
3. One who donates and wants others to donate
4. One who doesn't donate and doesn't want others to donate

As two and four don't actually donate, how can the beginning of the Mishnah call them donors to charity? The next Mishnah states that there are four types of people who go to the study hall:

1. One who goes but doesn't study
2. One who doesn't go but studies
3. One who goes and studies
4. One who doesn't go and doesn't study

---

5 Although most commentators say that it does actually mean in the future, it is the only verse that is not written in the future tense, so the simplest reading is in the present. See also Rav Tzadok, *Machshavot Charutz* 4.

6 Chap. 5:16–17.

Once again, how can numbers two and four be grouped as those who go to the study hall?

The answer is that every Jew at heart is a "donor to charity" and a "goer to the study hall." It's just that some of us aren't actually doing it.

Ultimately, we are pure spiritual beings, and once we can identify as that and live from that place, we can override our natural tendencies and manifest our divinity in the world. Rather than creating health, connection, holiness, and joy, our job is to strip away everything that's covering it up, revealing our true, already pure essence.[7]

The Jewish approach to character refinement is based on the verse, "ללכת בכל דרכיו—to walk in all His ways."[8] The Talmud[9] teaches that just as Hashem is merciful and compassionate, so too we must be merciful and compassionate. The most striking example of this comes in *Parshat Vayeira*, where the Torah says that Hashem appeared to Avraham while he was sitting at the entrance to his tent.[10] Unlike every other place in the Torah in which Hashem appears to someone, the verses don't tell us what Hashem said. It appears that Avraham and Hashem weren't even communicating; they were just sitting in the Highest state of Divine meditative communion (similar to what the Buddhists call *samadhi*). Then, suddenly, Avraham spots some dusty travelers, tells Hashem to hang on for a second, and rushes to wash their feet and feed them.

Rather than creating health, connection, holiness, and joy, our job is to strip away everything that's covering it up, revealing our true, already pure essence.

Seems a bit rude to me. If the point of doing the mitzvah of greeting guests is to be on a high spiritual level and connect to G-d, then Avraham was already at the highest level and didn't need to do a mitzvah to connect.

Yet we see that's exactly what he did. The Talmud[11] teaches that "גדולה הכנסת אורחין מהקבלת פני שכינה—it is greater to welcome guests than to

---

7 For more on this, see *Getting to Know Yourself* (דע את עצמך) by Rav Itamar Schwartz.

8 *Devarim* 10:12.

9 *Shabbat* 133b.

10 *Bereishit* 18:1.

11 *Shabbat* 127a.

welcome even the Divine Presence." Rav Noach Weinberg taught that from this story we see that the Jewish ideal for us in this world is not to be *with* Hashem in some sort of spiritual bliss, rather, it's to be *like* Hashem, to be Divine. The more we are *like* Hashem in this world, the more we'll be *with* Him in the World to Come.

The more we are like Hashem in this world, the more we'll be with Him in the World to Come.

The Rambam teaches that the mitzvot themselves were given to "subjugate one's evil inclination and improve one's character. Similarly, most of the Torah's laws are nothing other than advice from the Creator to improve one's character and make one's conduct upright."[12]

There are many examples of this in the Torah. In *Parashat Mishpatim*, we are told that when we see an enemy struggling we must go and help them, not allowing our prejudices (even if they are well-founded) to get in the way of doing the right thing. We must abandon our hatred, resentment, grudges, envy, anger, and hurt in order to rise to the level of manifesting Godliness in the world.

I used to find it strange that the Torah commands us to feel a certain way. Telling us to put on tefillin, light candles, eat matzah, I get. I can do that even if I don't feel like it. But to command us to feel something—to love G-d, to feel more joy at certain times, to not bear a grudge—just didn't seem to make sense at all. How can one be commanded to feel something?

What the Torah is teaching us is that in the long term, we can indeed be in control of our emotions, not suppressing or denying them, but fully experiencing them and reshaping and developing them in a healthy way. Many people excuse their mistakes and character flaws by claiming, "I'm only human." There may be something to that, but the reality is that we aren't only human. We have negative thoughts, speech, and actions, but they don't define us—they are, as the Alter Rebbe teaches in the *Tanya*, just garments for the soul that need to be cleaned in order to express the true essence of our being in this world.

12 *Hilchos Temurah* 4:13:
כדי לכוף את יצרו ולתקן דעותיו ורוב דיני התורה אינן אלא עצות מרחוק מגדול העצה לתקן הדעות ולישר כל המעשים.

The Torah is training us to go beyond our human nature, to manifest our Divine nature, our Godly soul.

So how are we going to start implementing real growth in the area of character traits? Rav Yisrael Salanter himself said that to change one trait is harder than learning the whole Talmud.[13] We may not be able to completely uproot our character traits, but we can certainly begin to stop them from playing such a strong role in our lives.

Try out these Enlightened Jewish Master character refinement techniques.

David HaMelech taught the path to refining character traits and all spiritual growth when he said, "סור מרע ועשה טוב—Turn away from evil and do good."[14]

What evil must we avoid?

Identifying with negative character traits. A girl once told me she hates herself. When I asked why, she listed a few negative character traits. I said, "I hear that, but those are your negative character traits you need to work on, they aren't you. If your kids have negative character traits, you won't hate them, so don't hate yourself for yours!" Never beat yourself up about negative character traits. That is a trick of the *yetzer hara* to disempower you. No one ever improved by beating themselves up. David HaMelech said, "*Ivdu et Hashem b'simchah*," spiritual work has to be done with *simchah*—putting ourselves down never works.

Rather than saying, "I'm an impatient person," and being resigned to that, say, "I have impatience," and consciously work on it.

Dwelling on negative thoughts. Negative character traits manifest through thought patterns, which then create emotions and then sometimes actions. An angry thought makes us feel anger,

13 I heard that he actually said it is more difficult than learning the *Pnei Yehoshua*, which is notoriously difficult to learn.

14 *Tehillim* 34:15.

which may make us shout or hit. To get away from the evil on one level means to stop saying and doing negative things (even if you are thinking and feeling them), but on a higher level, it means to be conscious when the negative thought itself is arising and choose not to give it significance. When you feel anger or impatience arising, be mindful enough to catch it early, take a deep breath, experience it fully, and let it pass. Don't fall back into entertaining the thoughts that will arouse and perpetuate the emotion.

Then comes the *aseh tov*:

Replace the negative thought.

- Every time you notice your mind putting you down, smile and say either, "That's not true," or, "Thanks for pointing that out, I'll work on it."
- Every time a jealous, impatient, or anxious thought arises, don't judge it or judge yourself. Don't try to escape it or make it significant in any way. Just acknowledge it and let it go. Smile and say, "You can't get me anymore."
- Replace the negative thought with a positive thought. For example, if you have an envious thought, list three things you appreciate in your life (if you really appreciated your life, you'd never be envious). If you catch your mind judging someone, think of two good things about them, and so on. After a while, the *yetzer hara* will stop throwing those thoughts if it sees you transforming them to positivity.
- Make a list of the negative character traits you need to let go of and start consciously working on them—read books, go to seminars, seek advice, and start to implement what you learn. Take small steps. Embrace the challenging situations that arise, which give you opportunities work on these traits.
- Start acting like someone with good character traits. The *Sefer HaChinuch* famously says:

> *You must know that a man is acted upon according to his actions, and his heart and all his*

> *thoughts always follow after the actions that he does—whether good or bad, and by doing good deeds we become good.*[15]

Therefore, if you are not so generous, force yourself to start giving more of your time and money to others. If you raise your voice often, train yourself to speak calmly. In this way you will retrain your traits.

- Finally, black-belt level once again is building *emunah*. If we truly integrated the knowledge that everything that happens is for our best, we wouldn't ever feel jealousy, anger, fear, or any other negative emotion. One way to develop *emunah* is to speak about it all the time. For example, when something "bad" happens, I take a deep breath and say, "Wow. Who would have thought this is the best thing for me? If I wrote a list of the top hundred best things for me, this wouldn't have been on it. Shows how much I know!" Even though I don't feel it at first, it makes me smile and helps implant the correct thoughts into my mind. We learn this from a verse in *Tehillim*: "האמנתי כי אדבר,"[16] which can be read as, "I built up *emunah* because I speak about it all the time."[17]

And the measuring stick of your success? *Simchah*. The only things standing in the way of us feeling innate joy are our own negative character traits. The more we fix them, the happier we become. We see once again

If we truly integrated the knowledge that everything that happens is for our best, we wouldn't ever feel jealousy, anger, fear, or any other negative emotion.

---

15 Mitzvah 16:
ולבו וכל מחשבתיו תמיד אחר מעשיו שהוא עוסק בהם אם טוב ואם רע כי מתוך הפעלות כי האדם נפעל כפי פעלותיו הטובות אנחנו נפעלים להיות טובים.

16 *Tehillim* 116:10; said in *Hallel*.

17 This is the interpretation of the Rebbe of Lechovitch.

that searching for happiness outside of ourselves is futile. All it really takes is a shift in attitude toward life.

It was actually in this area of character traits that I started to question the coherence of what I was learning through the Buddhist sources. I was wandering around the temple grounds one day in Vang Vieng, Laos, contemplating the teachings: on the one hand, the importance of nurturing love, compassion, and sympathetic joy, but on the other hand, not to get attached to anything of this world.

The question arose: How can I be truly loving and compassionate if I am also meant to be detached? Surely compassion involves some amount of attachment to the one I feel compassion toward, and love involves some sort of intrinsic connection. I realized that far from being detached, it's through knowing that we are deeply and intrinsically connected that these feelings can arise. Although I asked my masters and searched through the many answers to the paradoxical idea of detached compassion, none of them really sat well with me. I realized I still had a lot of searching to do if I was to find a fully coherent path to cultivating the character traits I needed to develop on my journey to true Enlightenment.

The only things standing in the way of us feeling innate joy are our own negative character traits. The more we fix them, the happier we become.

After a while in Vang Vieng, I decided it was time for a real adventure, off the beaten track and away from the backpacker trail. I took a bus up north to its last stop, got off in a small town, and asked around for the way to villages in the mountains. I packed a few provisions and set off, not sure where the trail would take me or what lay in store over the mountain passes. I used to say that you're not really living unless you have dirty feet. As I looked down at the blackened toes sticking out of my sandals, I smiled contently. Nothing felt as good as being on the solitary trail to who-knows-where. I walked through a couple of villages, where all the kids ran out to say hi and ogle the strange apparition walking through their neighborhood. None of the villages had running water or electricity; the only water source was a brown river that they bathed in, drank from, went to the bathroom in, and used for cooking. As I left each village, the kids would escort me on my way until their parents called them back to finish their chores or have something to eat. After walking about twenty kilometers up into the hills, I arrived in a village about two hours before dark and decided it would be best to find a place to settle in for the night. Curious faces popped out of the hut windows as word got out that a *farang* was in the village. I found out later that I was the first foreigner most of them had seen. At five foot eight, height isn't my greatest asset, yet in the village, I stood a good head above the tallest person there. After partaking for more than a week in their diet of stringy mushrooms picked from the river banks, on a bed of sticky rice, I realized that malnutrition had really stunted their growth.

The chief invited me into his hut, and soon word got out that there would be a gathering at his house for all the villagers. The whole community crowded around as I sat on the porch and addressed them. I'm not sure they really understood what I was showing them when I pulled out my well-worn map of their country on which their village obviously didn't appear, and as my camera wasn't digital, they had to remain a little confused about what I had done to them with the little metal box I carried with me. We sat drinking the rancid local rice wine through bamboo straws, and the villagers began to ask me questions. "Do you have mountains in your country?"

"Yes, big mountains," said I, melodramatically, throwing my arms in the air.

"Are there many *farang* in the world?"

"Yes, many." It carried on like this for about an hour before it started getting late and the crowd began to disperse. That night, as I settled into my sleeping bag on the wooden floor of the chief's hut, bag under my head as a security measure against thieves as much as for use as a pillow, I started pondering life. These people basically never left the village. They had no education, health care, or passports. They spent the majority of their waking hours farming and collecting water and wood in order to cook the food they farmed, so that they could eat, to stay alive, just to repeat the same cycle the next day. It seemed rather meaningless to me. After work they would sit around drinking and telling stories, playing games, and otherwise entertaining themselves to fill the time. I wondered if they ever stopped to think about the purpose of it all. Then it hit me that it wasn't that much different where I came from! Many people are stuck in a cycle of going to a job that doesn't particularly fulfill them and then spending their free time entertaining themselves, without ever stopping to ask themselves what the point of it all is. The quality of life is definitely better and more comfortable where I come from, and the entertainment is more entertaining—but in the end, people go through a similar cycle of just working to be alive and then getting whatever temporary pleasure they can in their free time. It became clear that the answer to my search for purpose was not to be found in the world I had come from, nor in the almost diametrically opposed lives of the people in the village. I still had a long way to go on my warrior's journey to discovering and fully living in line with the true purpose of life.

CHAPTER 5

Korea

Black Belt on a Paradise Island

Snow balancing precariously on the outstretched leaves of palm trees lining the coastal roads; ripe, deep-orange citrus fruits, with glistening ice caps, thriving in mikan[1] groves; Hallasan, the once fiercely active volcano, which still dominates the island, swathed in a frosty white carpet; frozen streams running through forested valleys like paths left by snails across the lawn; Christmas lights and overly decorated trees adorning the shop fronts of Seogwipo City; schoolchildren wrapped in hats, scarves, gloves, leg warmers, and earmuffs, carefully hurrying home on the icy pavements. Jeju-do, which was my home for just over a year, was magnificently showing that even in midwinter, it is one of the most spectacular places in the world.

After nearly a year and a half in Thailand and Laos, I felt the strong drive to move on to fresh pastures, face new challenges and adventures, experience an unfamiliar culture with different scenery, and ultimately start seriously pursuing my dream of training in martial arts. One day, while browsing a TEFL[2] website, I was attracted by a headline—"Come

1 A type of sweet mandarin found mainly in Korea, Japan, China, and South Africa.
2 Teaching English as a Foreign Language.

Teach English on a Paradise Island." I contacted the *hagwon* (after-school academy) that had posted the vacancy, sent in my CV, had a phone interview, was offered the job, and within two months arrived at my new home on "Honeymoon Island."

Lying one hundred kilometers off the coast of South Korea at the convergence of the Yellow and East China Seas, Jeju-do really is a paradise island and possibly the most phenomenal place I've ever lived. Dominated by Hallasan, the tallest and one of the three most sacred mountains in Korea, the island, which was created entirely through volcanic eruptions, is home to a stunning array of natural wonders. It boasts one of only eleven waterfalls in Asia that fall directly into the sea, over 360 *oreums* (mini-volcanoes), one of the longest and best-preserved underground lava tunnels in the world, and a mysterious road on which bottles and cars out of gear (seem to) roll uphill.

Then there are the idyllic beaches lining the coasts; intriguing rock formations called *dol hareubangs*—three-meter-high carved statues of unclear origin, said to give the power of fertility, and protection from demons; parks and gardens full of thousands of species of flowers and plants; waterfalls hidden in the depths of the forest, which covers over 10 percent of the island; and one of the biggest Buddhist temples in the world. Jeju-do, although officially part of Korea, has its own distinct culture, dialect, and very rich body of local myths and legends.

After taking a couple of days to settle in, I walked into Jong Il Hagwon for my first day of work and was met with a rather disturbing scene. A chubby eleven-year-old-boy was in the push-up position, with Mrs. Park, the headmistress, standing over him shouting, half a pool cue raised in her hand. She turned around when she heard the door open, and her eyes lit up when she saw who it was. She gave me the sweetest smile you could imagine through her bright-red, lipstick-smeared mouth, turned back around, and gave the boy one firm strike on his behind with the pool cue, probably much lighter than he would have received had I not walked in just then.

She then invited me to join her in the office, proceeded to explain the rules of the school, gave me a timetable, textbooks, board markers, and my own half pool cue, which she assured I could use whenever I saw fit. Unfortunately, I very often felt the need to use it; however, I took my frustration with the kids out on my desk instead, which made a loud enough sound to get everyone's attention without leaving red marks on their bodies.

In my free time, I'd cruise around the island on my motorbike with some of the other English teachers, enjoying the beaches and waterfalls, hiking the forest trails, playing tennis, visiting various temples and shrines, learning martial arts, and climbing Hallasan, the volcanic centerpiece of the island. There were teachers from Canada, Australia, and America, and we formed a tight-knit group of expats. Many of them were Christian missionaries, and I became very friendly with a pair of Mormons. I once attended a "cell meeting," where some passages from the New Testament were discussed, hands were held, and songs were sung. I went to a few great concerts at a hip progressive church in the neighboring town, where some of my colleagues from work were performing, and I became top scorer for the local Presbyterian Church football team. Seogwipo had been one of the host cities for the 2002 Football World Cup, with the likes of Germany and Brazil gracing the turf at its new $120 million stadium. Football had become a craze on the island since then, and new teams were springing up all the time, not least of all in the church league. I got connected to the team through one of my students and once again created strong friendships through the "beautiful game." My career came to an abrupt end when the captain of the team excitedly announced that there was an island-wide church tournament and the final would be played at the World Cup stadium. Based on our results in the league, we had a good chance of making the final, but the captain came up to me and said that to qualify for the team I'd have to come to church every Sunday. Out of nowhere, that same inexplicable drive that caused many nonreligious Jews to give up their lives rather than bow to an idol or eat pig kicked in. I told him that Jews can't go to church and so I'd have to sit out of the tournament, hence my own little Sandy Koufax[3] moment.

---

3 Legendary Major League Baseball Hall of Famer in the 1950s and '60s who opted to sit out of Game 1 of the 1965 World Series, as it fell on Yom Kippur.

Although Jeju still has a strong local culture and traditional feel to it, South Korea, unlike Thailand and Sri Lanka, is definitely a "first world" country—a term defined by Wikipedia as "democratic, capitalist, economically stable, technologically advanced, and with a high standard of living." Going in the face of those who say that money is the root of all evil, I could see lots of good that came from it—health care; education; welfare for more disadvantaged people in society; much lower rates of poverty, unemployment, and homelessness, to name but a few. Yet on the other hand, in contrast to the developing countries I had just come from, the first-world one I was in now definitely demonstrated the corrupting effect of consumerism on individuals and society. There was markedly less emphasis on community and familial closeness, and even though the standard of living was higher, there was far less contentment and happiness among the people. Along with this drive for modernity came another consequence. Although the older generation were still deeply imbued with a sense of tradition and love of the local culture, the young had been completely taken over by American culture. Hip-hop and baseball had taken over *minyo* and taekwondo as the most popular music and sports, and Christianity was the new religion for the spiritually progressive youth.

Of course, that didn't stop me. As with everywhere else I went, I was fascinated with the local culture, history, and tradition. Once I had perfected Jeju-satori (the local dialect), I refused to speak mainland Korean when there was an equivalent local word. I still spent many hours meditating in local temples, and, rather than wield my half pool cue to punish those who misbehaved in class, I would make them stay behind after class for *myongsang jikan*—meditation time. At first my students found it amusing (or annoying), yet after a while I saw them begin to feel infused with a love of and pride in their island culture. When they saw me on the street, they'd say, "*Yogie Jeju-Saram onda*—Here comes the Jeju Man!"

For me, coming back to the developed world after spending a couple of years in Sri Lanka and Thailand really highlighted the fact that "developed" is in many ways a terrible misnomer. We may have progressed economically and technologically, but society seems to have gone in the opposite direction. It was clear that the emphasis on capitalism and hedonistic pleasure was not creating better, happier, or healthier individuals. I started to wonder whether there was any way to have the best of both worlds—finding a balance between having financial stability and high physical quality of life, while still living with healthy and wholesome values that promote the physical, emotional, intellectual, and spiritual well-being of individuals and society as a whole.

It was only several years later, while learning Rabbi Dessler's classic work, *Strive for Truth*, that I found the answer. All it would take was a small shift in human consciousness and attitude to create the balanced and healthy individual and society we all hope for. Until then, I'd just have to continue playing the rather absurd role of middle-class Westerner with Thai villager values, living as traditionally as I could on a Korean Island, where the locals were striving to become Westernized! It was a role that I relished playing at the time but was far from the community and values I envisioned living with in the long run. My journey of striving for the truth was still very much underway.

> *Whoever dies with the most toys wins.*
>
> Malcolm Forbes

> נתון תתן לו ולא ירע לבבך בתתך לו:
>
> *You shall repeatedly give (to the poor), and your heart shall not be grieved when you give to him.*
>
> Devarim 15:10

Notwithstanding all the growth, beauty, and human goodness we find in the world, something has gone horribly wrong. Society is functioning on an extremely low level of consciousness. There is war, an absurdly unbalanced distribution of wealth and resources, abuse, depression, and we are destroying the planet by polluting the seas and chopping down the forests. What's going on here? Where did it all go wrong?

The problem really begins with people chasing happiness in the wrong places. We have an innate drive toward pleasure and away from pain and have developed the erroneous belief that what will bring the most fulfillment and pleasure in life is material wealth. This is because, to some extent, material possessions certainly do increase happiness levels. If you are homeless and cold, acquiring a small apartment and getting some hot food will certainly make you happier. If you have to ride your bike up lots of hills to get home from work after a hard day, buying an electric bike will give you great pleasure. Yet the truth is that once we have the basics, adding material possessions will never actually fulfill our emotional, intellectual and spiritual needs. In fact, quite the opposite is true. Research has shown that this focus is what causes most mental and emotional problems because wanting more than we need and comparing ourselves to others means we will never feel fulfilled, satisfied, and significant. One report shows that until an income level of $75,000 per year, happiness levels increase, but from then on, having more money makes absolutely no difference.[4]

Unfortunately, acquisition and material gain have become the highest values in society. Take a second now to imagine what a very successful person looks like.

If you are like most people, you pictured someone with a nice car, house, suit, and haircut. Success in Western secular society, whether anyone personally believes it or not, is usually defined by superficial, external values: what you have, how much of it you have, and what you, your things, and your partner look like. Magazines, TV shows, and movies glorify wealth and physical beauty, and the education system is geared toward building a career rather than good character.[5]

In his 2010 documentary *I Am*, Tom Shadyac[6] points out that in the Native American culture, someone who hoarded things was considered mentally ill. He goes on to demonstrate that hardly anything in nature takes more than it needs. The redwood tree drinks the amount of water it needs to stay healthy, the lion kills only one deer at a time. Humans

---

4 Study from Princeton University, reported in *Time* magazine, Monday, Sept 6, 2010.

5 See Ken Robinson's excellent TED Talk about how schools kill creativity.

6 Director of *Ace Ventura*, *Bruce Almighty*, and other films, who, after having a near-death experience, had an epiphany about life and made a documentary about what he discovered.

are one of only two things on the planet that are crazed about hoarding and acquiring beyond our needs. The other one is cancer. Cancer destroys everything around it, eventually killing off the organism that is keeping it alive. It appears that we are doing the same to our planet. The Torah says, "Hashem put Adam in the garden to work and guard it,"[7] and the Midrash[8] comments, "Be careful not to spoil or destroy My world, for if you do, there will be nobody after you to repair it," and yet we are going a long way toward destroying the world by abusing it and taking from it in an unsustainable way.

It's important to note that according to Jewish teachings, there is nothing wrong with being rich and having nice things. If you study and work hard, you deserve possessions to enjoy, and it is noble to provide for your family. Some philosophies teach that we shouldn't have money—it corrupts you, makes you greedy, causes worry, makes you arrogant, and makes you partake of things you shouldn't partake of. Although, unfortunately, this is often the case, it doesn't have to be like that. Many of our greatest sages (including Moshe Rabbeinu and Rabbi Yehudah HaNasi) were very wealthy. Many mitzvot, such as tzedakah, *maaser*,[9] *hachnasat orchim*,[10] and *pidyon shevuyim*,[11] are accomplished with money, so the money itself is clearly not the problem. The real problem comes when people start making money their top value at the expense of other people and the world around them, defining themselves and their self-worth by it. The World Watch Institute reports that the amount of money spent annually in America on cosmetics is eight billion dollars, and that an extra nine billion dollars a year would provide clean water and sanitation to all people in all developing nations throughout the world. Consumerism is consuming us and the world around us.

Consumerism is consuming us and the world around us

Ultimately, this ego-based, self-gain hierarchy of values is not only causing personal

7 *Bereishit* 2:15.

8 *Kohelet Rabbah* 7:28.

9 Giving ten percent of your income to charity.

10 Having guests.

11 Redeeming captives.

suffering and environmental catastrophes, it also causes abuse and suffering between people. When we value our own wealth, power, and physical pleasure over that of other people, we will inevitably cause suffering in the world.

So what's the answer? How can we start healing and stop harming the planet and the people on it? It should be no surprise to anyone that one of the key paradigms for perfecting ourselves and the world around us, as shared most famously by Rabbi Eliyahu Dessler, is the absolute reverse of the acquisition trend we see nowadays. Rabbi Dessler divides the world up into *givers* and *takers* and urges us all to move strongly away from being a taker, acquirer, and consumer, feeding our own ego-desires, toward becoming a conscientious and passionate giver.[12] He even identifies the desire to take as "the root of all evil in the world," and from what we learned above, we can see how this plays out. We need to start moving from "What's in it for me?" to "What can I do for others?"

One of the "less good" people in the Torah was a man called Korach, who started a rebellion against Moshe. The Torah portion starts with the words "ויקח קרח—And Korach took," but then completely fails to mention what he took. Many commentators have given answers to what he took, but in a sense, it doesn't matter what he took. The fact was he was a taker, feeding his ego rather than supporting others, was his real problem. His fate was certainly fitting, as he was ultimately swallowed up by the earth—the consumer became the consumed.

Success in Torah terms is not based on what you have, it's based on who you are, how much you have perfected yourself in thought, speech, and action, and how much you give to those around you. The Torah is full of admonitions to perfect oneself and help others, and ultimately to become a *tzaddik*, a fully righteous person.[13] The Talmud teaches that before a child is born, he is administered an oath to "be a *tzaddik* and not a *rasha*."[14] This means that our area of free will is in choosing good

12 *Michtav M'Eliyahu*, volume 1, *Kuntres HaChessed*.

13 Although there are a few definitions of what it means to be a *tzaddik* (see Rambam and *Tanya*), I'm just using it as a general term for a righteous person.

14 *Niddah* 30b.

over evil, perfecting ourselves over feeding our ego and physical desires, and being a giver and not a taker. In fact, a large amount of Torah law deals with how to treat others, fairness in business, correcting our character traits, and making sure everyone in society has the opportunity to similarly work toward the goal of reaching their potential and helping others. "צדק צדק תרדוף—You shall surely chase justice," "ואהבת לרעך כמוך—You should love your fellow as yourself," "לא תקום—Don't bear a grudge," "לא תטור—Don't take revenge," and "לא תחמוד—Don't covet," are some of the many Torah laws that exemplify the above. Not to mention feeding the vulnerable, fighting jealousy, hatred, and anger, giving tzedakah and *maaser*, and so on.

When asked by someone wanting to convert to teach him the Torah while standing on one foot, Hillel famously replied,

> דעלך סני לחברך לא תעביד זו היא כל התורה כולה ואידך פירושה הוא.
>
> *That which is hateful to you, don't do to others—that is the whole Torah, the rest is just commentary.*[15]

The Talmud teaches that "in the beginning Hashem clothed Adam and Chavah, and at the end He buried Moshe,"[16] demonstrating that the Torah itself begins and ends with acts of kindness. The list goes on and on. We see this beautifully manifested in the Jewish attitude toward rights and obligations. Rabbi Akiva Tatz points out that "modern society is largely concerned with rights. The highest code of such societies is their Bill of Rights. In striking contrast is the Torah, the Jewish Constitution. The Torah never mentions rights, only obligations!"[17] Why is this? He goes on to share that rights and obligations always come together. My right to life is your obligation not to kill; your right to property is my obligation not to steal. However, there's a huge difference in which one you focus on. Rights are egocentric, what is owed to me, whereas obligations shift the emphasis to what I can do

15 *Shabbat* 31a.

16 *Sotah* 14a.

17 Rabbi A. Tatz, *Worldmask* (Jerusalem: Targum, 1995), "The World of Obligation," pp. 100–106.

for others, on being a giver; not what's in it for me, but what I can do for others. Relationships and societies built on this attitude are happy and healthy.

Beyond just building a better society, Judaism teaches that there is actually a whole higher reason for becoming a selfless giver. *Chessed* (loving-kindness/unconditional giving) is such a central attribute that David HaMelech teaches us that the world was built upon *chessed*,[18] while the Ramchal teaches in *Derech Hashem* that the whole purpose of Creation was so that Hashem could bestow His *chessed* on His creations. As we spoke about in the previous chapter, our lives are about tapping into and manifesting our Godly nature. So just as Hashem is a Giver, it is only by being givers ourselves that we can achieve this goal and channel the flow of *chessed* that comes from Him. Just like water in a pond becomes stagnant if it isn't taking in and giving out, so too, we as human beings start to deteriorate if we aren't reaching out to others around us.

Rabbi Itamar Schwartz teaches that just doing a kind act for someone, although it is certainly a mitzvah and a good thing to do, is not called *chessed* unless it was an expression of love, or done with the intention of building love![19] The whole point of *chessed* is to foster or reveal the intrinsic connection between the giver and receiver. Therefore, when the Ramchal teaches that Hashem created the world to give *chessed* to His creations, it means to reveal the intrinsic, loving connection we have to Him. In fact, it is through our acts of *chessed* that we bring Creation to perfection. The Midrash[20] teaches that Turnus Rufus asked Rabbi Akiva, "What is better, the work of G-d or the work of man?" He was making a protest against circumcision, asking how it was possible to desecrate G-d's handiwork. Rabbi Akiva showed him some wheat and some bread and said, "Aren't these (bread rolls) better than the sheaves?" Hashem provides us with the raw materials and asks us to partner with Him in uplifting the world to perfection.

---

18 *Tehillim* 89:3.

19 *Getting to Know Your Soul*, chap. 7, "*Chessed*: Kindness."

20 *Midrash Tanchuma, Parashat Tazria* 5.

Then comes black-belt-level giving. Many people will tell you that there is nothing we can give to Hashem. He is perfect, so He needs nothing. Although this is certainly true on the highest level, our Sages teach us that He set up Creation in a way that He does, so to speak, need us. In *Tehillim*,[21] David HaMelech tells us, "תנו עז לאלוקים—give strength to Hashem." How exactly do we do that? What strength could we possibly give Him? Several sources teach that although Hashem's existence is not at all dependent on our believing in Him, He, so to speak, has no way to be manifest in the world if we don't recognize His existence.

Pirkei D'Rabbi Eliezer[22] asks, "אם אין עם מקלסין למלך אי זה הוא כבודו של מלך—If there are no people to praise the King, where is the glory (or honor) of the King?" When we consider this alongside the verse in *Yeshayahu*,[23] "מלא כל הארץ כבודו—The world is full of His glory (or honor)," we see that this is only true if we praise Him. We are the ones who bring His honor in to fill up the world!

We find another phenomenal source for this idea in the Torah portion of *Chayei Sarah*. Avraham calls Hashem "אלהי השמים ואלהי הארץ—G-d of the heavens and G-d of the earth,"[24] but just a few verses later, he calls Him only "אלהי השמים—G-d of the heavens."[25] Rashi, commenting on the second verse, shares a Midrash that teaches that Avraham said:

> *Now He is G-d of heaven and earth, as I have familiarized Him in the mouth of the people (they speak about Him). But when He took me from my father's house, He was G-d of the heavens but not G-d of the earth, for those who lived in the world did not recognize Him.*[26]

---

21 *Tehillim* 68:35.

22 Chap. 3. Similarly, in his commentary on *Bereishit* 38:30, Rabbeinu Bachaya shares the famous dictum, "אין מלך בלא עם—there is no King without a nation."

23 *Yeshayahu* 6:3.

24 *Bereishit* 24:3.

25 Ibid., 24:7:
אמר לו עכשיו הוא אלהי השמים ואלהי הארץ, שהרגלתיו בפי הבריות, אבל כשלקחני מבית אבי היה אלהי השמים ולא אלהי הארץ, שלא היו באי עולם מכירים בו, ושמו לא היה רגיל בארץ.

26 The word for recognize is *makirim*, from the same root as *hakarat ha'tov*, used in relation to Adam earlier in *Bereishit*.

Only once Avraham had spread G-d-consciousness in the world could Hashem truly be said to be here.

> *It is told that the Chassidic master, Rabbi Menachem Mendel of Kotzk, once asked his students, "Where is Hashem?" They seemed a bit confused at the simplicity of the question, and answered that He is everywhere. The Rebbe looked at them and said, "No. He is wherever you let him in."*

That we are here as partners with G-d and have something we can give Him (so to speak) is a radical and awesome idea, truly exceptional among world religions. Far from being somewhat insignificant sinners trying to ingratiate ourselves in the eyes of G-d or trying to reach a state of unity with G-d through secluded meditation, Judaism teaches that Jews, once we become givers, are necessary Divine partners in the journey toward the perfection of the universe.[27]

From the last two chapters we see a paradigm shift in the definition of success. Success, in Torah terms, is not based on what you have, it's based on who you are, how much you have perfected yourself in thought, speech, and action, and how much you are giving to those around you. When imagining a successful person, what should come to mind is not someone with lots of money. A successful person is a *tzaddik*—someone with refined character traits, a good attitude and disposition, someone who is there for others and always does the right thing.

We all know this intuitively because at every funeral, the eulogies focus on good character traits and how much the person contributed to the world around them, not on how many cars they had and how much money they made. What we are aiming for, how we get self-respect, what creates a meaningful life, and what dictates how much *simchah* we have is not how much we make but how much we give. It's not about how we've prospered but rather how much we've grown.

---

27 See also Rav Kook's incredible teachings on *shleimut* and *hishtalmut* in *Orot HaKodesh*.

It's not about looking good, it's about being good. Healthy self-esteem comes from respecting ourselves for how much we've grown and contributed, not what others think of us based on superficial values. Reaching success in these terms is the key to living meaningful, constructive, and happy lives.

Try out these Enlightened Jewish Master healthy self-esteem and real success tools.

Self-Esteem. Too many people nowadays are down on themselves, with their self-critical voice running wild. The truth is that you must give yourself permission to love yourself for no reason, even though you aren't perfect. *Pirkei Avot* teaches that "כל אהבה שהיא תלויה בדבר בטל דבר בטלה אהבה—any love that is dependent on something, when that thing ceases, the love ceases," meaning, it wasn't real love in the first place. I love my wife and kids for no reason other than they are my wife and kids. They don't need to perform or do anything to receive my love, and there is nothing they can do to make me not love them. The same goes for ourselves. We don't need a reason to love ourselves, and nothing we do should make us stop loving ourselves. Ultimately, we are pure, perfect *neshamot*—what is there not to love?! Healthy self-esteem, however, is based on what we like and respect about ourselves, and how we manifest our soul in the world through our good choices, values, achievements, and character traits.

- Write a list of ten things you like about yourself, are proud of yourself for, and ways in which you help others. Keep adding to the list.[28]
- Sit up straight, breathe deeply and go through the list, taking time to actually feel good about these things. (Remember, just like with the gratitude list, for real depth

28 Watch your mind try to sabotage this exercise—every time you think of a good trait, it will find examples of when you weren't perfect in that area, or throw negative traits at you. Acknowledge your *yetzer hara*—say, "That is true, and I'll work on those things, but for now I'm focusing on the positive."

and transformation we need to take our intellectual awareness and start to feel it in our heart. Lists don't help if we aren't "experiencing" them.)

Be a giver. Change your attitude from "What's in it for me?" to "What can I do for others?"; from "She's not pulling her weight in the relationship" to "How can I pull my weight more?" (even if they aren't pulling theirs! Yeah, I know it's not fair, but Enlightened Jewish Masters aren't so worried about what's fair, they care about what's right). Do this by being aware when "taker" thoughts arise. Smile at them and replace them with "giver" thoughts.[29]

- Give yourself a target of three acts of giving a day. That could be time, money, compliments, space, gifts. Always look for opportunities to reach out to help people.

I know it's not fair, but Enlightened Jewish Masters aren't so worried about what's fair, they care about what's right.

Make decisions based on this question: "Which of these options will help me grow most and contribute most to those around me?" (This isn't always black and white, but the answer is usually the one that takes more effort. Sorry.)

Understand that we have two powerful drives. One is to look good and feel good. This comes from our animal side (*nefesh ha'behamit*), looking for physical and ego pleasure. The other is to be good and do good. This comes from our Godly side (*nefesh Elokit*). Whichever one we feed will become stronger. The truth is that if we chase feeling good and we attain what we desire, we actually end up feeling not so good. Once we stop chasing "looking good and feeling good" and rather focus

29 Obviously, you shouldn't be taken advantage of. Sometimes (although not so often—so don't use this as a justification not to give), what people need the most is for you to stop giving to them so they can learn to appreciate you and life more.

on "being good and doing good," we'll actually end up feeling really good about ourselves (and looking good in the eyes of others). In this way we live a meaningful and therefore joyful life. This is real success. The beautiful irony is that rather than by increasing what we have, it's by perfecting ourselves and giving to others that we fulfill that innate drive for pleasure in life in the highest way, moving from temporary ego pleasures to higher emotional, intellectual, and spiritual ones. Once we achieve this attitude shift, we'll be able to live a balanced life of financial stability and high standard of living, without compromising the values and attitudes that create healthy, happy individuals and societies, just as the Torah has been guiding us toward all along.

It was on Jeju Island that I finally started my real martial arts training. One of my students introduced me to her taekwondo master, and from that day on, a beautiful master-student relationship developed. I went for private lessons with Oa-Sabomnim (Master Oa) for an hour and a half every morning. He was a very sweet and simple man, born and brought up on the island, fiercely proud of his culture, and endearingly interested in mine. After training, we'd often go out into nature, jumping into freezing waterfalls, scrambling up mountain paths, and would sometimes meet up at night in one of the many fried-chicken and beer joints downtown to practice each other's respective language, which was pretty challenging, seeing as when I arrived he couldn't speak one word of English (and when I left he could only speak about three), and my Korean only became really conversational after about three months. It's incredible how two people who love and respect each other and want to connect can connect so deeply even without being able to put together one full sentence.

After a few months, due to lack of students, Oa-Sabomnim had to close his dojo, so we joined forces with his friend, Kwanjangnim (grand master). Kwanjangnim was a huge man, well over six feet tall, former high school national taekwondo champion, and although he had put on a bit of a belly in his later years, he still had the most deadly pair of legs I've ever had the misfortune to be repeatedly kicked by. Many a time a kick onto the pads he made me hold for him would actually lift me slightly off the ground and send me rolling backward a couple of feet. Training included jumping through hoops to side-kick wooden boards in half, jumping off walls, spinning in the air to kick a board and land all on the same foot, punching out candles without touching them, practicing *pumsae* (forms) over and over again, and *georoge* (sparring). Looking back, I have no idea how I ever managed to do it all without breaking an ankle or worse. With the daily intensive training, plus an early morning run and meditation, and a gym session after work, it took me a year and two months to get a black belt, significantly less than it takes in England, probably because they train far less and the masters would definitely be sued if they treated their pupils like we were treated in Korea.

On the day I got my black belt, Oa-Sabomnim and Kwanjangnim took me out for a special meal to celebrate. It was a very pricey and fancy restaurant that served local traditional specialties, with traditional music playing, traditional décor, and waiters in traditional dress. As we tucked into our meal, downing soju and singing local folk songs at full volume, I reveled in the fact that I'd finally found the perfect fusion of modern opulence and traditional culture.

Yet the next day, while floating in a rock pool of crystal-clear water and looking up at the cloudless blue sky near my apartment, relaxing on a day off from training, I suddenly felt that there was something missing in my life. I realized that I had everything I could want on my paradise island, apart from one thing—the opportunity to really be there for other people, to give of myself and my time to improve the lives of those around me. Everyone on the island was well-fed and educated (or at least had the opportunity to be), and society was running very well on the whole. At that point I decided that it was time to move on, back to the developing world, back to places that on the one hand are so alive and rich and deep in culture, yet on the other are struggling so heavily with poverty and other forms of deprivation. I didn't have to think long about where the next stop might be. The time

I realized that I had everything I could want on my paradise island, apart from one thing—the opportunity to really be there for other people.

had clearly come to fulfill my dream of visiting the former stronghold of the British Empire, home of the yogis and ascetics striving for moksha (liberation or enlightenment) in the foothills of the Himalayas or the plains of Tamil Nadu. It was time for me to hit the vast subcontinent of India. When my contract at the hagwon came to an end, I packed my bags, bought a one-way plane ticket, and within a week I stepped out of the airport into the stifling heat of New Delhi.

CHAPTER 6

India

Fasting, the Dalai Lama, and Yoga by the Ganges

On arrival in India, I went straight to McLeod Ganj, a small village half an hour up a very windy road from Dharamshala in the northern province of Himachal Pradesh. It's the main home of the Dalai Lama and the Tibetan people in exile (and, more recently, the Israeli backpacker in exile). When I say straight there, I mean after a pretty crazy fifteen-hour, winding, potholed, overnight bus ride from Delhi, which, to be fair, by Indian standards is actually not that long. In the foothills of the Himalayas, the air is crisp and fresh, and the sky seems to stretch up higher than in other places. Birds of prey circle overhead, and the valley stretches miles out to the plains below. Colorful prayer flags flap in wind, Tibetan schoolchildren stand on street corners in their immaculate blue uniforms; monks with shaven heads and red robes bustle through the streets talking on their cell phones. Meditation is much easier there; the atmosphere just brings it out of you. Spiritual consciousness pervades the whole place.

I settled into a guesthouse overlooking the valley and noticed that next door was a center where people were paying to take part in special fasts for seven days. The idea of paying for a fast didn't make much sense to me, but for some reason the idea of a seven-day fast did. And so, for the next week I sat on the roof of my guesthouse, where I partook of one very thin slice of papaya and drank two cups of water a day, as I sat reading Eckhart Tolle's classic mindfulness book, *The Power of Now*. On the fourth day of my fast I heard that the Dalai Lama was in town and was giving a talk that afternoon. To get the strength to walk the two and half hours up the mountain, I added a slice of apple to my diet (which didn't exactly give me that much more energy) and set off, water bottle in hand, to hear some words of wisdom from the person known as one of the world's greatest spiritual leaders, Tenzin Gyatso, the fourteenth incarnation of Avalokiteśvara, the Buddha of Compassion.

I arrived in the midst of a huge festival of around three thousand Tibetans—street performers, food vendors, traditional musicians and dancers, monks, animals, and hundreds of kids colorfully clad in their best clothes running around excitedly, waiting for their leader to appear. The Dalai Lama finally showed up and proceeded to give a forty-five-minute speech—completely in Tibetan!

I wasn't amused. Lack of any real nourishment for four days, plus exhaustion from climbing the mountain, coupled with the amazing local dishes that everyone was so generously offering me but of which I could not partake, in addition to the total lack of any understandable inspiration from the man himself left me somewhat dispirited (to say the least), and I set off for home in not the greatest mood. I moved slowly through the crowds and finally left the noise behind as I began my descent to Mcleod Ganj.

And then it happened.

I was halfway down the forested path as the sun was setting over the mountainous horizon, when out of the blue it hit me in the most stunning and clear way—The Power of Now!

> *"See if you can catch yourself complaining, in either speech or thought, about a situation you find yourself in, what other people do or say, your surroundings, your life situation, even the weather. To complain is always nonacceptance of "what is"... When you complain, you make yourself into a victim... The*

pain that you create now is always some form of nonacceptance, some form of unconscious resistance to "what is."[1]

I stood there for a few awesome minutes as the sun shone gently on my face through the trees, feeling total presence and bliss, having truly tapped into the power of accepting "what is." I almost floated the rest of the way back to my guesthouse, and spent the next three days on a spiritual high, as the hustle and bustle of life in this busy haven of locals and spiritually seeking travelers unfolded around me. As I sat on the roof, water bottle in hand, watching the eagles soar, silhouetted against the sunrise and sunset over the Kangra Valley, I enjoyed what actually felt like enlightenment, or at least the closest I had come yet.

Anyone who has experienced the multi-sensual, visceral, geographical, cultural vastness that is the Indian subcontinent knows that no one can really do it justice in one chapter of a book—even the longest one—but I'm going do my best.

By the time I arrived there three years into my journey through the East, I was deeply entrenched in the spiritual search, on a quest for the truth of reality, ultimate consciousness, self-knowledge, the mystical experience, enlightenment—known by the locals as moksha, liberation.

Looking back, I'm not sure why I thought my Self could be hiding somewhere in an ashram in India, but like many Western Jews, I knew it couldn't be back in the life and values I'd left behind, nor in the religion of my birth, which seemed so outdated, rigid, and unspiritual.

After two months in McLeod Ganj and Bhagsu,[2] I decided it was time to move down the valley to Rishikesh, the yoga capital of the world, considered one of the holiest cities in India. It is most famous in the West as the location of the Beatles Ashram, where John, Paul, George, and Ringo spent time with their guru, the Yogi Maharishi Mahesh, in February 1968. While there, they composed around thirty songs, including John

1 E. Tolle, *The Power of Now* (Namaste Publishing, 2004), chap. 4.

2 The next village, two kilometers up the mountain.

Lennon's "Happy Rishikesh Song." The ashram itself is now deserted, overgrown, and rundown—a perfect playground for troops of Hanuman langur monkeys, with their shiny silver coats, black faces framed with white fur, and long wiry tails. These huge beasts rise up intimidatingly on their hind legs, reaching taller than a man, and are not afraid to grab a bag of nuts or other food out of the hands of unsuspecting tourists.

Rishikesh is spread out on both banks of the River Ganges, which at this point is close to its source high in the mountains and is usually crystal clear and ice cold. "Mother" Ganges is considered a god by the Indians, and many thousands of people take a purifying dip in her every morning and evening, even though by the time it reaches Varanasi, around a thousand kilometers eastward across the plains of Northern India, it becomes, to quote *The Economist*,[3] a "brown soup of excrement and industrial effluents" and is "not considered safe for bathing." During my time in Varanasi, I saw at least two dead cows and a dead human floating down the river, no doubt on their way to their watery resting place in the Indian Ocean, another seven hundred and fifty kilometers across the dry plains of Bihar State.

Downtown Rishikesh is like any other Indian city—crowded, noisy, and polluted—not a place where the average person would want to spend too much time. Yet just two kilometers upriver, it turns into a strikingly colorful spiritual wonderland. Two huge suspension bridges, Ram Jhula and Laxman Jhula, built by the British, span the width of the Ganges, connecting the two banks, which are both crammed with ashrams, temples, *dhabas* (restaurants), postcard and incense shops, spiritual bookstores, travel agents, and internet shops, all catering to the bustling market of souls seeking enlightenment and peace of mind. Barefoot sadhus (ascetics) dressed in light-orange robes, Indian pilgrims from all parts of the subcontinent, polio-ridden beggars and street kids, European and Israeli spiritual seekers, and several cows and monkeys all bustle their way along the riverbanks and across the bridges, each looking for whatever will satisfy their particular hunger. Rishikesh is like a spiritual supermarket with an eclectic mix of courses on offer: yoga, tai chi, meditation, breathing

3 "India and Pollution: Up to Their Necks in It," *The Economist*, 27 July 2008.

workshops, massage, healing, Reiki, Indian music, Ayurvedic cooking, and chanting, to name but a few. After checking out the scene for a few days, I finally signed up for the intensive fifteen-day yoga retreat at Yoga Niketan, up on a ridge with stunning views of the Ganges.

Yoga is one of the more well-known paths to Westerners, although the asanas (body positions) so popular in the West are only one step on Patanjali's Eightfold Yoga Path.[4] Yoga means unification, and is an attempt to unify body and mind, individual soul and universal G-d. There are many different philosophies, ideas, and practices in India that have been conveniently lumped together by the West under the title of Hinduism. In reality, there is no one religion called Hinduism, and it's quite possible that several 'Hindus' may each believe very different things. The basic philosophies are thought to be ancient, with the earliest known holy book, the Rig Veda, written in around 1200 BCE (approximately 112 years after the giving of the Torah at Sinai in 1312 BCE). There are six orthodox schools that believe in the authority of the Vedas, yoga being one of them, and several nonorthodox schools that don't.

I was in my element in the course, learning discipline and self-control, understanding and experiencing the connection between mind and body, individual soul and universal consciousness. I used my free time each afternoon to take tabla[5] lessons on the banks of the Ganges, and every day at sunset I would join the *aarti puja*, a prayer service on the other side of the river, with *bhagans* (devotional hymns) and singing praises to the river, while floating candles down it to wash away sins and reflect on the day that had just passed. Aside from the physical postures and full body cleanses (I'll spare the details), I learned basic yoga philosophy, including the four main paths of yoga:

- **Karma-marga**—the path of action ensuring that all you do in the world is conscious and for a higher purpose.

4 The others are Yama—commitments; niyama—avoidances; pranayama—breathing techniques; pratyahara—cutting out the sense perception; and then three increasing levels of meditation: dharana, dyana, and samadhi—the final level being where the individual soul merges with the greater Divine soul.

5 A classical Indian drum.

- **Jnana-marga**—the path of intellect, involving understanding the nature of reality and the path of enlightenment through studying the ancient texts and writings of the masters.
- **Bhakti-marga**—the path of devotion, involving surrender to and love of the Divine through prayers and chanting and hymns.
- **Raja-marga**—the path of meditation, the art of quieting and focusing the mind, connecting to the Divine oneness permeating all of Creation.

Many afternoons I would sit meditating next to the Ganges, a simple meal of rice and curried potato wrapped in a banana leaf, tabla resting by my side, hardly any possessions or attachments to the physical world, no way to be contacted, no responsibilities.

I'd smile to myself, truly content, saturated with the feeling that I was tapping into the consciousness of the masters, ascetics, and sadhus, finally walking in the footsteps of the holy men of the past, following the path of the Yogi, uniting body, soul, and Divine soul in the ongoing dance of life.

> *Renunciation! Renunciation! You must preach this above everything else. There will be no spiritual strength unless one renounces the world.*
>
> *Swami Vivekananda*[6]

> *A person will one day give reckoning for everything his eyes saw that, although permissible, he did not enjoy.*
>
> *Jerusalem Talmud, Kiddushin 4:12*

In some ways, Vedanta, possibly the main Indian philosophical schools, started out teaching a similar mystical worldview to that of

6 A key figure in the introduction of the Indian philosophies of Vedanta and Yoga to the Western world, circa 1890.

Judaism.[7] In brief, there is the infinite, eternal Divine Creator.[8] All of Creation is a manifestation of the Oneness of this Being, distinct yet not separate at all, because if anything was separate from G-d it would mean that G-d isn't infinite. On one hand, the Divine is totally beyond the Creation and unaffected by it, i.e., transcendent (the universe is in G-d). This is why Hashem is often referred to as "HaMakom—the Place," the space in which everything exists. At the same time, the Divine is the "material" of all Creation and is totally within it, i.e., immanent, as the famous Kabbalist Rav Moshe Cordovero said:

> *The essence of Divinity is found in every single thing—nothing but it exists. Do not attribute duality to Hashem. Realize, rather, that Hashem exists in everything. Do not say, "This is a stone and not Hashem." Rather, all existence is part of Hashem, and the stone is a thing pervaded by Divinity.*[9]

The logical consequence of this is that our soul—*neshamah* in Hebrew, and *atman* in Sanskrit—is a pure, manifest piece of Divinity referred to as "*chelek Elokah mi'ma'al mamash*"[10] in Jewish sources, and "*tat tvam asi*" in Sanskrit, distinct but not separate from the whole. As Rabbi David Aaron says so poetically, "You are someone—you are some of the One!" This philosophy is called panentheism (not to be confused with pantheism, which teaches that the universe is just G-d and G-d is the universe and nothing more).[11]

---

7 There are actually a few different schools of Vedanta: Advaita, Vishtadvaita, and Madhavadvaita, to name a few, with some significant differences in philosophy, but for the purposes of this chapter I'm keeping it simple and general.

8 Of course, the Divine Creator is more than infinite and eternal. Infinite means unlimited in any way, including spatially—the Divine Creator created space—while eternal means going on forever in time—but the Divine Creator created time. They're just the best words we have.

9 *Shiur Komah* to *Zohar* 3:14b, *Idra Rabbah*.

10 See *Tanya*, part one, chap. 2.

11 Panentheism is the belief that the Divine interpenetrates every part of the universe and extends timelessly (and spacelessly) beyond it. Unlike pantheism, which holds that the Divine and the universe are identical, in panentheism, the universe and the Divine are not ontologically equivalent. God is viewed as the soul of the universe, the universal spirit

When I first arrived in yeshiva, the rabbis I shared the Eastern mystical philosophies with were very interested, but not all that surprised. They showed me at the end of the Torah portion of *Chayei Sarah* that around 437 years before the writing of the Rig Veda, in 1637 BCE, Avraham sent six of his sons "eastward to the East country" with gifts. We learn that these were gifts of certain spiritual wisdom and ritual practices, which may have shaped the philosophy of the East. There are many examples I have come across that support this idea. One example is that the name of the creator deity is Brahma, and he has a consort named Saraswati, which is strikingly similar to Avraham and Sarah. Legend has it that Saraswati was created when Brahma took a piece of his own body from which he fashioned her—which once again sounds familiar to me. These are just a couple of many examples I've come across, which may be just a coincidence, although we don't really believe in coincidences.[12]

Although parts of the core philosophies are similar, or at least were in the past, in practice the two religions are very different indeed.

When I first arrived in yeshiva, the rabbis I shared the Eastern mystical philosophies with were very interested, but not all that surprised.

Firstly, Hindu philosophies have been mixed with local animist and spiritualist religions, have personified the Divine energies, and have created a pantheon of deities that people now worship and even attribute individual power to. This, of course, is antithetical to core Jewish beliefs and practices, which teach that there is no power apart from Hashem and it is forbidden to make, let alone worship, any statue or image. The other major way the two paths differ is in our relationship to the physical world. Hindu philosophy teaches that this world is *maya*, an illusion. Not unlike the Buddhist idea of detachment, these philosophies in general expound that the

present everywhere, in everything and everyone, at all times (Wikipedia).

12 In fact, the Hebrew letters of the word for coincidence, מקרה, can be rearranged to spell "רק מה'—only from Hashem," "ה' רקם—G-d embroiders," "קרה מ'—happened from Hashem," and, of course, "קרמה—karma" (the law of Divine justice as taught in Hindu philosophy).

way to achieve moksha (liberation) is to renounce attachment to the physical world, freeing ourselves from the shackles of the body and ego, which pull us down, control us, and ultimately keep us from connecting to our Divine essence. Like Buddhist monks, Hindu sannyasins don't get married, they refrain from physical intimacy, generally eat as little as is needed to sustain the body, renounce all worldly pleasures, have no money and very few possessions, and live ascetic lifestyles, free from the stresses of everyday life and able to concentrate on meditation, yoga, and other spiritual practices.[13]

Whereas Eastern philosophies in general teach us that to be spiritual we have to detach from the world, and the West tends toward materialism and physicality, Judaism teaches that we need to balance and integrate the physical and the spiritual aspects of ourselves—our body and our soul.[14] Our Sages teach that rather than being a physical being (a body) that is trying to have a spiritual experience and connect to our soul, we are in fact spiritual beings (soul) that have a body, the aim of which is to use physicality as a tool to becoming spiritual.

At first glance, as is very often the case, it seems that Jewish sources actually teach two opposing ideas in this area.

On the one hand, we learn that G-d wants us to partake fully in and enjoy the physical pleasures of the world. Two of the first things Hashem says to Adam and Chavah are "*Peru u'revu*—Be fruitful and multiply,"[15] and, "*Mi'kol eitz ha'gan achol tochel*—Eat of all the fruit in the garden."[16] Our festivals are accompanied by lavish meals, we are meant to have special clothes for special occasions, and Purim takes indulgence in physicality to the next level. The Talmud teaches that a *nazir*, one who refrains from drinking wine, must bring a sin offering at the completion of his term because we aren't meant to separate from

---

13 There are some esoteric schools that are more focused on the physical world and the path of the householder, however, in general, the ideal is renunciation, as seen by the opening quote from the highly respected guru Vivekananda.

14 Maybe this is why Israel is in the middle of the East and West.

15 *Bereishit* 1:22.

16 Ibid., 2:16.

worldly pleasures.[17] The above quote from the Jerusalem Talmud even suggests that at the end of our time here we'll have to answer for not enjoying the physical pleasures of the world. So we see that Judaism teaches that Hashem, like any loving father, wants His kids to enjoy some ice cream once in a while.

On the other hand, other sources teach us that "the way of Torah is to eat bread with salt, drink a little water, and sleep on the floor,"[18] and Rebbi[19] claimed that he derived no pleasure from the world, even in his little finger! The Talmud[20] teaches that we should sanctify ourselves by abstaining also from that which is permitted to us, and the Rambam teaches that we should only eat what we need to maintain our health. [21] The *Zohar* calls this world *alma d'shikra*, a world of falsehood, and the Ramban teaches (in seeming contrast to the Talmud above) that the real reason a *nazir* brings a sin offering when he finishes his time as a *nazir* is because he

> *turned away from his special holiness and service of Hashem. It would be proper for him to vow abstinence forever and remain all his days a nazir and holy to Hashem his G-d…so he requires atonement for returning to be contaminated by the desires of this world!"*[22]

From this it is clear that self-centered pleasure-taking is not the way either.

Of course, these two ideas are not contradictions, and taken together they demonstrate the true path. Judaism teaches that the ultimate spiritual path is not to shun the world and remove ourselves from it, nor to get lost in materialistic hedonistic pursuits. Rather, in order to be on a truly high spiritual level, we need to be very fully in this world, just in

---

17 *Nedarim* 10a.

18 *Avot* 6:4: כך היא דרכה של תורה פת במלח תאכל ומים במשורה תשתה ועל הארץ תישן.

19 Rabbi Yehudah HaNasi, redactor of the Mishnah, in *Ketubot* 104a.

20 *Yevamot* 20a.

21 See Rambam, *Hilchot De'ot* 3:2.

22 Ramban, *Bamidbar* 6:14:
כי האיש הזה חוטא נפשו במלאת הנזירות, כי הוא עתה נזור מקדושתו ועבודת השם, וראוי היה לו שיזיר לעולם ויעמוד כל ימיו נזיר וקדוש לאלוהיו כל ימי נזרו קדוש הוא לה' והנה הוא צריך כפרה בשובו להיטמא בתאוות העולם.

such a tremendously mindful way that we actually use physicality as a tool to become connected to the greatest spiritual heights.

How is this achieved? Let's take eating as an example. We love eating, and a major part of almost every festival and holy day is the *seudat mitzvah* (the mitzvah meal). However, before we put any food in our mouth, we make sure it's kosher; if it's dairy, we work out when we last ate meat; we say a specific blessing; we eat consciously (or at least are meant to); we share words of Torah during the meal; and we conclude with a specific blessing. In this way, we turn eating itself into a spiritual practice. The same goes for all other permitted physical pleasures in the world. Physical pleasure for its own sake is egotistical, temporary, and it disconnects us from spirituality. Pleasure as the reward for or consequence of yearning to uplift the world and bring G-d-consciousness into all mundane activities is the greatest, most authentic physical pleasure there is.

Still, there is a catch. In the *Mesilat Yesharim*, the Ramchal teaches that to get to the level of *kedushah*, holiness, which includes getting pleasure from the world, we first have to go through the level of *prishut*, separation from it. To achieve the level of being able to turn our physical pleasures into a spiritual act, we first have to have reached the level of being able to eat bread and salt, drink a little water, and sleep on the floor, while still remaining joyful and connected. The Lubavitcher Rebbe teaches this idea from the donkey that appears in *Tanach*. The verse in *Parashat Shemot*[23] tells us that "Moshe took his wife and sons, rode them on *the* donkey, and returned to Egypt." Rashi comments that the Torah, by saying *the* donkey, is referring to a specific one. "It is the donkey that Avraham saddled for the binding of Yitzchak, and it is the one upon which the Mashiach is destined to be revealed."

The Rebbe explains that this teaches us about our relationship to physicality. The word "*chamor*—donkey" shares the same root as the word "*chumriut*—physicality." He says that the process is to first

---

23 *Shemot* 4:20, Rashi: חמור המיוחד, הוא החמור שחבש אברהם לעקידת יצחק והוא שעתיד מלך המשיח להגלות עליו.

"saddle," i.e., subdue, our physicality, at which point we can "ride" it, i.e., use it for holy purposes, and then in the times of Mashiach, Godliness will actually be revealed through the physical. [24]

In other words, once we have broken (or at least controlled) our need for and addiction to physical pleasure, we can partake of it in a truly conscious way without relying on or being controlled by it.[25]

The problem is therefore not the pleasure itself, it is the תאוה, the craving for it. *Pirkei Avot*[26] teaches in the name of Elazar HaKapar that "הקנאה והתאוה והכבוד מוציאין את האדם מן העולם—strong desire for physical and ego pleasure removes a person from the spiritual world," while the third paragraph of the *Shema* warns us, "ולא תתורו אחרי לבבכם ואחרי עיניכם—Do not chase after your hearts and eyes." Furthermore, the Talmud states that "אין אדם עובר עבירה אא"כ נכנס בו רוח שטות—a person doesn't ever sin unless he is overtaken by a spirit of folly."[27] The Lubavitcher Rebbe[28] asks what exactly this spirit of folly is, and answers, "זו תאוה—it is physical desire!" This means that every mistake we ever make, every time we don't act in line with our souls, it's because we are drawn to the pleasures of the physical world. Seemingly, we can have and enjoy pleasure, but not as a way to fulfill our craving for it.

Once we have reached the level of not being so drawn to physicality, we can reach the level of *kedushah*, holiness.

I've heard many people say, "All religions are just different paths to the same idea; you have to be a good person." Very sweet, but not true. I don't need G-d to come out of the heavens to tell me to be good—it's just basic common sense, and there are plenty of good atheists walking around.

---

24 Heard first in a *shiur* by Rabbi Yanky Tauber, based on a Chassidic discourse given by the Lubavitcher Rebbe.

25 This process is known either as הכנעה (submission), הבדלה (separation), and המתקה (sweetening) in the writings of the Baal Shem Tov (*Keter Shem Tov* 28), or אתכפיא (subduing) and התהפכא (transformation), most prominently in Chabad Chassidut.

26 4:28.

27 *Sotah* 3a, in the name of Reish Lakish.

28 *Likutei Sichot* part 2.

Being good is the most basic level. Our Sages teach us that "*derech eretz kadmah la'Torah*—being a mensch is a prerequisite to keeping Torah." The actual goal of the Torah and mitzvot is to help take us to the next level: being holy. We see this time and again in our liturgy, where the words "mitzvah" and "holy" come together: "קדשנו במצותיך—Make us holy with Your mitzvot,"[29] "וקדשתנו במצותיך—You made us holy with Your mitzvot,"[30] "אשר קדשנו במצותיו—Who made us holy with His mitzvot,"[31] "עשיתם את כל מצותי והייתם קדושים לאלוקיכם—You will do all the mitzvot and be holy."[32] Furthermore, the Torah urges us, "קדושים תהיו כי קדוש אני ה' אלקיכם—Be holy because I am holy, Hashem your G-d."[33]

I've heard many people say, "All religions are just different paths to the same idea; you have to be a good person." Very sweet, but not true.

So what does it mean to be holy? Although the most common understanding of *kadosh* implies separation,[34] probably the most famous verse in which we find the word *kadosh* is, "קדוש קדוש קדוש ה' צבאות מלא כל הארץ כבודו—Holy Holy Holy, Hashem, Master of Legions, the whole world is filled with His glory!"[35]

That doesn't sound separate to me. In fact, it sounds totally present and immanent. This suggests that to be holy means to have the balance between being fully present and involved in the world, while also transcending it in the sense that we are not to be controlled or defined by it; rather we interact with physicality in a conscious and soulful way. As the verse above teaches, just like Hashem is holy, i.e., totally beyond the world (transcendent) yet totally within and involved in it (immanent), so too must we be.

This, however, is no easy task, and it is because of the pitfalls of trying to walk this path that many religious philosophies stress renunciation

---

29 Shabbat *Amidah*.

30 Rosh Chodesh and Yom Tov *Amidah*.

31 Blessing over doing a mitzvah.

32 *Shema*.

33 *Vayikra* 11:44, 19:2.

34 Rashi, *Vayikra* 19:2.

35 *Yeshayahu* 6:3, said as the pinnacle of the daily morning and afternoon prayers.

of the physical. It just seems too hard to be involved in the world without getting sucked in. Human nature is to be pulled toward physical desires such as food, and ego desires such as honor. Therefore, many philosophies prefer to just withdraw completely.

The truth is that without some sort of guidance and system it *would* be almost impossible to achieve this balance of physicality and spirituality. It is for this reason that Hashem had to give us the Guidebook—the Torah—the instruction manual that teaches us how to tread the fine line between these seemingly opposite forces.[36] Far from being burdensome obligations that G-d has imposed on us, mitzvot are in fact physical acts that have been given to us as connection points through which, if done with intention and joy, we can reach the highest level of spirituality and truly connect to ourselves and our purpose: an intimate relationship with Hashem.[37]

> *There's a story about a Buddhist monk, a college student, and a rabbi, who each enter a room containing wine bottles free for the taking. The college student walks into the room, starts drinking and singing with delight until he finally starts crying about his life, throws up, and passes out. The Buddhist monk walks in and, noticing the effect of alcohol, undertakes never to touch a drop, and walks out. Then the rabbi enters. He sees the wine on the table, checks one of the bottles and sees that it's kosher, opens it up, and pours himself a glass. He takes a few moments to say a blessing, showing gratitude to Hashem, mindfully bringing G-d-consciousness into the act, thereby sanctifying the wine. He has a few sips and takes out the Torah book he has been learning and sees some ideas he hadn't grasped before. He has another glass, feels good, sings a few uplifting melodies before making an after-blessing, cleaning up, and leaving to go and give some charity.*[38]

36 See *Chovot HaLevavot, Shaar Avodat HaElokim*, chap. 2.

37 The word mitzvah itself is related to the root *tzavta*, connection.

38 Heard from Rabbi Benjamin Blech.

In moderation and with consciousness, the physical world can be enjoyed and sanctified. Physical pleasure is fine, it's the craving for it that is the problem, as our masters tell us:

> *It is well-known that the power of craving dominating the intellect is the beginning of all sin and the source of all disgrace.*
>
> *Chovot HaLevavot*[39]

> *Hashem placed us in circumstances where many factors distance us from Him. Those are physical cravings, which, if you follow after them, cut you off from the true good.*
>
> *Mesilat Yesharim*[40]

With this in mind, here are some Enlightened Jewish Master training exercises to help us break through *ta'avah* (craving) and reach *kedushah*. Like all spiritual growth, it's important to take small steps. The Ramchal himself teaches:

> *A person must be cautious in acquiring [the attribute of] "separation"*[41] *not to want to skip and jump to the other extreme all at once. For this will certainly not succeed. Rather, he should move gradually in separation, little by little, acquiring a bit today, and adding a bit more tomorrow, until he habituates so completely that it becomes like second nature to him.*[42]

---

39 Ninth Gate, "Gate of Separation"—מן הידוע כי הגברת התאוה על השכל היא ראש כל חטאת וסבת כל גנות.

40 Chap. 1:
והנה שמו הקדוש ברוך הוא לאדם במקום שרבים בו המרחיקים אותו ממנו יתברך, והם הם התאוות החמריות אשר אם ימשך אחריהן הנה הוא מתרחק והולך מן הטוב האמיתי.

41 The ability to control, if not completely overcome our craving for completely self-centered pleasures.

42 Chap. 2, "Acquiring Separation":
וממה שצריך ליזהר בקניית הפרישות הוא, שלא ירצה האדם לדלג ולקפוץ אל הקצה האחרון שבו רגע אחד, כי זה ודאי לא יעלה בידו, אלא יהיה פורש והולך מעט מעט, היום יקנה קצת ממנו ומחר יוסיף עליו מעט יותר, עד שיתרגל בו לגמרי, כי ישוב לו כמו טבע ממש.

So try just one of these exercises a week. Let's focus on eating, as this is our most basic physical desire.[43]

Breaking *ta'avah*: Anything you *really* crave ("Those fries smell amazing"; "I just need some chocolate"), just don't have it. Eventually, the pleasure you get from being strong and not giving in to your cravings will be much stronger than the temporary pleasure you'd get from eating the chocolate. You could buy it for Shabbat as a treat for doing so well during the week.

The Rambam[44] says you should eat whatever is good for you, whether you like it or not, and refrain from things you do like if they are not good for you. With this in mind:

- DHD! Don't have dessert. You aren't hungry and it's not good for you.[45] You only want it for the three minutes of physical pleasure it will give you. You gain much more from refraining. Start with one day a week or one time a day, and build up from there.[46]
- Try eating some healthy food you *davka* don't like. Whatever someone gives you to eat that's nutritious, just eat it.
- At a restaurant, decide what you want most, then order something else. (Or let someone else order for you).
- Take one plate of food and that's it. No refills.
- Leave some food over. Make sure it's a nice bit that you really want.

---

43 With all of these exercises, if you can't do them *b'simchah*, it may be better not to do them at all for now, especially if they are going to cause resentment, moodiness, *shalom bayis* or relationship issues, big financial loss, or if they will ruin your day, your learning, or your work.

44 *Hilchot De'ot* 3:2: לא יאכל כל שהחיך מתאוה ככלב וחמור אלא יאכל דברים המועילים לגוף אם מרים אם מתוקים ולא יאכל דברים הרעים לגוף אע"פ שהן מתוקים לחיך. See also ibid., 5:1.

45 The *Mesilat Yesharim* points out that no animal would choose to eat something it knew wasn't good for it—especially if it wasn't hungry!

46 Eventually, you could build up and become a member of DOOS—Dessert Only on Shabbat (and festivals/special occasions). This has the huge added bonus of increasing *oneg* and *kavod Shabbat*.

Building *kedushah*:

- When eating something you really like, relate the pleasure of the taste back to its source. Feel wonder and gratitude toward Hashem.
- Take the craving for the food and redirect it toward yearning for Hashem. In this way, the *ta'avah* itself is transformed and uplifted into *ahavat Hashem*![47]

The Ramchal even uses the word *ta'avah* to teach that "*ahavat Hashem* is when one truly longs for and craves (מתאוה) the closeness of Hashem."[48] This idea is beautiful expressed in the song *Yedid Nefesh*, which teaches that "יערב נא ידידותך מנפת צוף וכל טעם—connection to Hashem is sweeter than nectar and any other taste."

After spending so much time in meditation retreats, yoga courses, fasting, and sitting in caves and temples, following my breath going in and out, I started to get the feeling that sitting in a beautiful place, separated from the problems of the world, trying to overcome my ego while so many people were suffering around me, was, well, a little egotistical. It seemed clear to me that the world couldn't have been created for us to overindulge and abuse it, but it also didn't make too much sense to me that the actual goal was to completely renounce it. There had to be a balance. At the time, the balance that spoke to me most was to live a simple, spiritual life of meditation and peace in the Indian countryside, while running an orphanage to help the lives of as many vulnerable kids as possible. Little did I know that, even though it was a truly noble plan, so much more than that would soon be asked of me…

If I had more space I'd finish this chapter by telling you about the two months I spent in Bodhgaya—the town dominated by the temple built next to the Bodhi Tree where Buddha was enlightened—where I

47 See *Sefer Baalei HaNefesh L'haRaavad*, "*L'tzorcha u'l'ha'naata.*"

48 *Mesilat Yesharim*, chap. 18, "*Chassidut*": והנה ענין האהבה הוא שיהיה האדם חושק ומתאוה ממש אל קרבתו יתברך.

volunteered in Samanwaya Orphanage, run by Dwarko Sudrani, a fascinating man not least of all because he was Gandhi's last living disciple.

I'd share some of the conversations I had late into the night with Suresh-ji—who had devoted his life to caring for the thirty kids in his orphanage in Baghar—and about the time the Naxalite-Maoist freedom fighters who were terrorizing the state came to him to seek advice in the middle of one of our chats about the benefits of yoga for the kids. When they left he shared that he was very glad they hadn't kidnapped me as he'd expected them to.

I'd tell you about my time down south in the ashram of one of India's most famous gurus, where I happened to be when the huge tsunami struck India, Sri Lanka, and Thailand—which I only found out about four days later when I checked my emails and saw one from my father to all the heads of the Indian states asking for any news of my whereabouts.

I'd tell you about my trip to Manali, where I got stranded on a mountain with a dreadlocked sadhu who suddenly became paranoid and wanted to rush home in the middle of the night, meaning I had to charge down the ragged rocks behind him with only a makeshift torch made of his shirt wrapped around a branch dipped in some highly flammable substance and set alight to show us the way. I'd tell you about the burning bodies on the banks of the Ganges in Varanasi; my near-death experience in the thick fog that descended suddenly on Triund Mountain; my visit to a local Indian hospital in Pondicherry, where an injection made me vomit and made my whole arm swell up like a tennis ball, as tens of bleeding and moaning Indians lay on the floor all around me.

I'd fill you in on thirty-five-hour train journeys, high-altitude hikes to swim in lakes, rivers, and waterfalls, and the time I almost got stuck up a mountain for two months as a freak blizzard blocked off all roads and footpaths leading back to town.

Yet, as I said at the beginning, India is too vast to be squeezed into one chapter of a book, even the longest one. Suffice it to say, it taught me in so many ways the lesson of accepting what is, as it is. In India you can neither fight against nor run away from the reality, the heart-wrenching poverty, the breathtaking beauty.

It was only much later that I discovered that there could be an even higher level of enlightenment, a higher level of acceptance of "what is," a step above the Power of Now.

The Talmud[49] teaches us that not only should we accept "what is" because that's the reality, but that everything that happens is actually for our good, specifically orchestrated by a Loving Guide in order to help us grow and reach our potential and purpose in life. The key is not to just accept "what is," but to understand fully and feel deeply that "what is" is absolutely the best possible thing for us, however difficult it may seem on the surface. In this way, we not only avoid suffering from it, we learn to embrace it and use it as our tool to achieve insight and growth. To know this and live it fully is the real enlightenment, the real power—the Power of *Emunah*.

After a few months in yeshiva, I was sitting on the roof of my dorm room, thinking back fondly to my time on the banks of the Ganges. I started to wonder if I had given up the real quest for holiness and spirituality and settled for something less. I had always felt Judaism was an outdated religion, void of spirituality and truth—an old man in the sky telling me what to do or he'd punish me, full of can't dos...

Had I lost touch with the ideological adventure seeker who wouldn't settle for less than the truth and the most peak experiences? Had I let go of that inspired, inquisitive part of me that craved connection, ultimate knowledge, the mystical experience? Had I given up my "Self" to do everything the rabbis, ancient and modern, tell me to do?

It took just a cursory look to assure me that quite the opposite was true.

The Judaism I encountered revealed to me that every moment is a meaningful new opportunity to connect joyfully and powerfully to the magic of life.

---

49 *Berachot* 60a.

I realized that the path I had chosen is a balanced synthesis, if not the basis, of all the yoga paths I'd learned about many years earlier. Conscious action (karma-marga) is laid out in the mitzvot, guiding us how to change ourselves and the world around us through giving charity, relating to our fellows in an honest and wholesome way, using the physical world as a tool to be spiritual. The intellect (jnana-marga) is pushed to the limit by Torah study, which sharpens the mind and perception of the world to an incredible degree through insight into the deep teachings of real masters. Yearning devotion (bhakti-marga) in three prayer services and over a hundred blessings a day; powerful, heart-moving *niggunim* (songs) in candlelit rooms as Shabbat goes out; personal prayer in forests and fields; and finally, deep meditation (raja-marga), as practiced by the masters of Kabbalah. Far from being the dull, ritualistic religion I had thought it to be, Judaism turned out to be the comprehensive path to consciousness, understanding, and self-realization, perfecting the self and the world around us, unifying our individual soul with the One great, Divine soul. In short, I discovered that Judaism is the Ultimate Yoga.[50]

The Judaism I encountered revealed to me that every moment is a meaningful new opportunity to connect joyfully and powerfully to the magic of life.

50 Yoga means unification, i.e., the realization of the innate connection between the *neshamah* and Hashem.

CHAPTER 7

China

Shaolin Masters and Survival Missions

James and I set off into the wilderness of Changbaishan, the mountain range that forms the natural border between China and North Korea, with just a five-by-two-meter sheet of plastic, four kilograms of rice, some noodles, two kilograms of kimchi, a packet of cookies, a couple of cigarettes, and a large machete that we bought at the Erdao Baihe Central Bus Station. Although we had both grown up in England, our childhood couldn't have been more different. A few years younger than me, standing at over six feet tall, with a long mop of ginger hair and a scraggly beard, James grew up in the English countryside, working the land with his hands, hiking the windswept mountains of Scotland, and going to church on Sunday—a far cry from my middle-class North London Jewish upbringing. And yet we hit it off the first time we bumped into each other, each wandering around the quaint former British hill station of Shimla in Northern India, looking for a place to watch the 2003 World Cup rugby final between England and Australia. After witnessing England's historic 20–17 victory on a small, fuzzy TV in a hotel lobby, we spent a couple of weeks traveling together, playing chess, hiking in the mountains, and volunteering in the orphanage in Bodhgaya.[1] We eventually went our separate ways, but stayed in touch, and when the chance for adventure arose in China, I knew he was the man to partner with. We had agreed that under no circumstances would

1 See chap. 6.

we return to civilization in under six days, even though we heard that a few weeks earlier, a foreigner had wandered off into the mountains and crossed into North Korea by mistake, where he was shot, or just arrested, depending on which version of the story you chose to believe. Either way, that was not on my bucket list. We entered the national park, and as soon as we were out of sight of the rangers, ducked off the main trail and ran through the undergrowth until we came to a small stream running down the mountainside, a runoff from the sacred Tianchi Lake that filled the center of the now-extinct volcanic crater. We crossed the stream, walked a bit further down into the valley until we found a perfect spot, and set about using our plastic and some wood to form a makeshift home. We created an A-frame shelter, with two branches forming the *A* at the one end, and a long crossbeam that we lay across the top and lodged into a tree at the other end. We draped the plastic over the structure and pinned it down on one side with some sharp wooden pegs we had carved with our machete, leaving the other side wrapped around a branch and unpegged so it could be lifted up and closed as desired—our own convertible tent. Then came the business of gathering as much grass as we could to cover the floor of our home, creating a comfortable natural mattress, while at the same time collecting wood for our fire, and branches and leaves to camouflage the structure from the prying eyes of park rangers and North Korean snipers (okay, so our imagination ran away with us a bit, but it was all part of the fun). As we set up camp, we could see the path winding its way up the crest of the mountain, with unsuspecting tourists coming back from the crater while we nestled in for the night.

And then it began. Slowly at first, then gradually building up to a consistent and monotonous downpour, as the Northeast China rains swept across the mountain and continued almost nonstop for the next three days. That meant no fire, which meant no heat or cooked food, leaving us to survive on one cookie and a couple of spoons of kimchi a day. It also meant very little exploring the area outside of short forays when the rain let up for a few minutes—seeing as we only had the clothes on our backs and no way to dry them.

We were pretty cold and hungry and didn't have much to do as we crouched in our meter-tall, five-meter-long enforced prison for a few days. Yet, unlike the weather, we were very far from downcast! This was it! We were living the dream, albeit not 100 percent as planned, but the dream nonetheless! Our friends were working in office jobs and here we were, in the middle of the mountains, surviving in the wilderness, being creative, with minimal rations, totally free and wild; two English boys pretending to be survival experts, us against the elements, maybe physically confined, but emotionally soaring over the mountains of one of the most mystical and stunning places on earth.

I arrived in China toward the end of May 2004, focused on pursuing my dream of martial arts training in the mountains that had seen centuries of enigmatic Taoist sages, real and mythical martial arts masters, and the rise and fall of several great Emperors and their dynasties. Shaolin, in Henan Province, is the world headquarters of kung fu. In the fifth or sixth century, Boddhidharma, an Indian monk, is said to have come to China. Upon seeing that the monks were constantly being robbed by groups of bandits, he decided to teach them how to defend themselves. Legend has it that he was meditating, gazing at a wall for nine years, when in the seventh year he kept falling asleep, so he cut off his eyelids and tossed them away over his shoulder. Where they landed grew the first green tea plant, leaves in the shape of eyelids, which produce tea that keeps you awake in a healthier way than having your eyelids removed.

I arrived in Deng Feng, a town about fifteen kilometers from the Shaolin Temple, at the foot of the holy Mount Song, where tens of martial arts schools cater to thousands of practitioners of many different fighting styles. I started asking around for the best schools and began hearing rumors of a picture-perfect temple up in the mountains, which housed a small kung fu academy. I expectantly made my way up the winding mountain roads for around two hours, when behold, rising out of the mist, I got my first glimpse of Fa Wang Si, the second-oldest Buddhist temple in China. Stretching up level after level into the Yuzhu Peak of Mount Song, Fa Wang Si, apart from housing a small martial arts academy, attracts thousands of tourists and pilgrims each year. On each level is a temple building with ornate banisters lining the stone staircases. Statues of fearsome dragons, lions, and demons protected the deities in the temples, large rocks made great meditation seats, and small lawns and sculpted bushes and trees added splashes of natural green to the Hollywood-movie-like setting.

Training began at 5:00 a.m., when the bell would sound to wake us from our all-too-short slumber, certainly not enough sleep to help our bruised and aching bodies recover from the grueling training of the day before. We began the new day with some stretching before traipsing down to the bottom of the mountain from where we'd begin our run back up to the temple. On the first day, I hardly made it a quarter of the way up before my lungs felt like they were going to burst and my legs refused to go any further. By the time I left five weeks later, I could comfortably make it all the way, and had cut my time by three-quarters.

Then we had breakfast, which, like lunch and dinner, consisted of very oily rice, fried eggs, and some stir-fried vegetables. The rest of the day was spent stretching; practicing cartwheels and flips; perfecting the five main animal forms—tiger, dragon, snake, crane, and leopard; weapons training (my favorite was the *guun*, or long staff); weight training; tai chi; and personal meditation. The master spoke almost no English, and my Mandarin never really got past the basics, yet he always managed to get his point across, often with a firm blow of his bamboo stick to the back of our thighs.

When we had some free time, we went exploring the mountainsides, found some small lakes to swim in, and at night we'd sometimes go into town for a beer and karaoke. But usually we were too worn out from the day's training to have the energy to make it down to town, so after dinner and a final training session, we collapsed into our beds in the cramped dormitory, exhausted yet exhilarated from another day of pushing our bodies and minds to the limit, conquering physical and mental obstacles—helping me live up to the Chinese name my master gave me, 和平战士, Heping Janshe, "Peaceful Warrior."

Don't pray for an easy life, pray for the strength to endure a difficult one.

Bruce Lee

לפום צערא אגרא—*According to the effort is the reward.*

Ben Hei Hei (Pirkei Avot 5:26)

In all walks of life, from martial arts to music, personal growth to business, we see that to achieve anything takes focus, discipline, personal sacrifice, and effort. In fact, a comfortable life—although fine—is never going to be extraordinary and memorable.

Take a sports person, for example. He watches what he eats, doesn't go out drinking with friends, gets up early, lifts weights, and does stamina training—day in and day out, he pushes himself to the limit to achieve his goal. That is the only way to success. My least favorite phrase in the English language is, "It's easier said than done." I don't dislike it because it's not true—it *is* true. It's just that the phrase is useless and defeatist, just a statement of fact, usually an excuse for not getting things done. Once, a guy in yeshiva asked me how he could lose some weight. I suggested going to the gym and focusing on cardiovascular workouts, doing high reps of lighter weights, cutting sugars and fats out of his diet. When he replied, "Wow, Rabbi, that's easier said than done!" I gave him a bit of a confused look and informed him that while indeed it is easier said than done, just saying it wouldn't help him lose any weight, whereas doing it most likely would.

A comfortable life—although fine—is never going to be extraordinary and memorable.

Life, especially a great one, is not easy and comfortable, although many of us would like it to be. All achievement comes from overcoming some sort of struggle. Rav Noach Weinberg taught that people mistakenly think that pain is the opposite of pleasure. However, the truth is that the opposite of pain is no pain, or comfort. Pain is often the price we pay to achieve true pleasure, as they say, "All growth comes from stepping out of the comfort zone." When we truly believe that something will give us pleasure, we are willing to put in the work and take great pains to achieve it, whether it's working hard for exams or going to the gym so we look good.

At some point in life, just like the sports person, people need to ask themselves what they value, what they are passionate about, what they are living for, and therefore what they are prepared to put effort into:

Do you want a healthy relationship with your spouse? That takes effort.

Do you want to be rich? That takes effort.

Do you want to raise well-balanced and happy kids? That takes effort.

Do you want to become a *tzaddik*? That takes effort.

You want to help people, find a fulfilling job, learn a language or instrument, climb mountains—anything really worthwhile takes effort.

Even people who claim to be a bit lazy are willing to put in the effort once they have a goal they value. I once asked a group of college kids if they found it hard to get up in the morning. They all raised their hands. "What if I offered you $50,000 to meet me at 4:00 a.m. and do ten star jumps, who would be there?" All hands went up again. So I pointed out that really none of them find it hard to get up, they just don't value what they're getting up for.

Anything really worthwhile takes effort.

The foundation of all discipline, and what therefore takes the greatest effort, is self-control. This means to be able to do, say, and even think what we know is right and healthy even when it's difficult and we don't feel like it.

The Torah, in the third paragraph of the Shema, exhorts us to develop self-control, telling us not to chase after our hearts and eyes,[2] just going along with however we feel and whatever we desire. We humans (unlike animals, who—unless there is an external factor—can't control themselves) don't have to eat just because we feel hungry, don't have to shout at our kids just because we're in a bad mood, and we can still go to the gym, even when we feel tired. Those with self-control can hold themselves back from doing detrimental things

---

2 *Bamidbar* 15:39.

and push themselves forward toward greatness, not just at the whim of their thoughts and desires.

The master of self-control, and the only person in the Torah whom we refer to as "HaTzaddik,"[3] was Yosef. The normal reason given for this is because he managed to overcome his physical desires in the incident involving his master's wife. This required a large amount of self-control, enabling him to overcome this most powerful drive in order to do the right thing. Yet there was another occasion where he demonstrated this trait to an even greater degree. As a young boy, he shared with his brothers the dream he'd had in which they all bowed down to him. This really upset them, and they ended up selling him into slavery. He went down to Egypt, where, after several trials, he rose up to become the second-in-command of the whole country. Many years later, there was a famine in Israel and the brothers were forced to go down to Egypt to seek food to bring back to Yaakov, their father. When they arrived in the palace, they bowed down to the viceroy of Egypt—who was, unbeknown to them, their brother Yosef—ultimately fulfilling the dream from all those years ago. At that moment, Yosef had the best opportunity of all time to say perhaps the four most satisfying words known to mankind: "I told you so!" It's an awesome feeling to be right, to have your ego boosted, to be the victor, especially after being betrayed. Yet Yosef held himself back from needing to feed his ego, from needing to be right. Instead, he only had their best in mind and didn't even blame them for their treachery. This is the sign of a true master, someone who has the discipline and self-control to do what is right, physically, emotionally, and spiritually in any situation.

We humans don't have to eat just because we feel hungry, don't have to shout at our kids just because we're in a bad mood, and we can still go to the gym, even when we feel tired.

On one level, and the way most people look at it, self-control means the ability to control one's thoughts and desires, to not just go with them and let them control us. However, that implies that the thoughts

3 Although there were many *tzaddikim*, he is the only one we call HaTzaddik.

and desires are my Self that I need to control. From a Torah viewpoint, self-control means that my Self, i.e., my soul, my true essence, is in control, making the decisions and overriding the thoughts and desires of my body in order to lead the way toward becoming a *tzaddik*. All we need to do is have the presence of mind in any situation to ask ourselves, "What would the best me, the soul-me, think, say, or do in this situation?" and act accordingly. To the extent that we manage to do this and act according to what our best selves dictate, we will reach success and true mastery in life.

It takes a lot of discipline to live the path of an Enlightened Jewish Master. It's not easy to get up before sunrise for davening every morning, to say one hundred *berachot* a day, and to hold back from eating certain foods, looking at and listening to certain things, and even thinking certain thoughts. For a Jewish businessman to give up a day of work a week, or a pregnant woman to pass up on the Ben and Jerry's after eating meat, is not a simple matter. Committing to do these things takes a strong will and value system and requires consistency and strength of character. Every effort we make is very dear and special in the eyes of Hashem.

Here are some training exercises to make sure we are putting in the effort to become real Enlightened Jewish Masters.

Get up like a lion. The first halachah in the *Shulchan Aruch* is: "יתגבר כארי לעמוד בבוקר—Be strong as a lion [to beat your *yetzer hara*] to get up in the morning (to serve Hashem)."[4] Getting up like a mensch is a complete game changer. It means you beat your *yetzer hara* in the first battle of the day, setting the right tone for the rest of the battles to come. The Kotzker Rebbe said that it's impossible to get up like a lion if you go to bed like a donkey, so make sure you go to bed envisioning getting up strongly in the morning, not dreading the sound of the alarm.[5]

4 *Shulchan Aruch* 1:1.

5 Don't look at your phone for at least forty-five minutes before going to sleep.

The halachah continues: "שיהא הוא מעורר השחר—That you should wake up the morning!" This means that, preferably, we should be getting up before sunrise—every Buddhist monk, Hindu priest, and really anyone who is living purposefully, gets up before sunrise.

The *Shulchan Aruch*[6] rules that "זמן תפלת השחר מצוותה שיתחיל עם הנץ החמה—The mitzvah of praying in the morning is to start with the sunrise!" So start getting up at least once a month to daven *neitz*.[7] Rosh Chodesh would be a good choice in order to start the month strongly.

The Baal Shem Tov says the difference between davening *neitz* and after *neitz* is like the distance from East to West![8]

Exercise: The Rambam tells us the importance of exercise in *Hilchot De'ot*:

> *Maintaining a healthy and sound body is among the ways of God—for one cannot understand or have any knowledge of the Creator if he is ill.*[9]

Therefore:

> *The rule is that he should engage his body and exert himself every morning until he heats up his body.*[10]

Choose a short exercise to do—ten push-ups a day, a brisk walk to work, a basic stretching routine. Start strengthening and enlivening your body—it gives you much more energy than a cup of coffee.

---

6 *Orach Chaim* 89.

7 If you can't do these things, e.g., daven *neitz* or cut out treats without getting arrogant, self-righteous, and looking down on others, it may be better not to do them at all. On top of this, whenever you are doing a special spiritual exercise, don't go around telling people. The fewer people who know the better.

8 *Tzvaat HaRivash* 16. Obviously, if davening *neitz* will destroy your learning or functioning during the day, or you are in yeshiva and there is the set minyan, don't push yourself. We should be moving toward this, though. Once a month shouldn't be a problem.

9 4:1.

10 4:2.

Make a list of things you should do more of and things you should do less of. Any time you think to yourself, *I really should get up earlier/call home more often/tell my spouse more often how much I appreciate him/her/exercise more/drink less coffee/spend less time on social media/find out how so-and-so is doing*...just do it! Pick up the phone, set the alarm, close the computer, whatever it takes. If you should do it, then do![11] You may need an "accountability partner"—someone who holds you to your goals.

It is certainly a high level just to have the self-control and commitment to do these things every day, yet the goal is not just about getting them done; it's about how we are doing them. The sign of a true Jewish master is that s/he is following the path not out of fear, guilt, or habit but rather with true understanding, consciousness, intention, and joy.

The sign of a true Jewish master is that s/he is following the path not out of fear, guilt, or habit but rather with true understanding, consciousness, intention, and joy.

If Fa Wang Si taught me one thing, it's that we won't achieve much while staying in our comfort zone. I still smile (and wince) as I remember my master's grinning face as he proudly shouted his only English phrase—"No pain, no gain, no pain, no gain!" before swinging, with relish, the bamboo stick toward the back of my already red, raw thigh.

On the fourth day, James and I woke up to silence. No rain pattering above our heads, no wind rustling the plastic walls of the tent. The sky was a clear blue and the sun warmed our faces as we emerged from our makeshift home. We stacked the wood up in a trellis format so the sun could dry it out with the help of the soft breeze that was now wafting over the mountainside. We washed off

11 For more tips on this, watch my class on YouTube called, "When Willpower Is Not Enough."

in the river, surveyed our surroundings, and breathed the fresh air of the calm after the storm.

We were excited to get a fire going and cook up our rice and noodles, but were a little concerned that the smoke might be seen from the trail. We gathered up our wood, cooking utensils, and the food and headed out into the next valley, where we nestled down and eventually got the fire started even though the wood was still pretty damp. Twenty minutes later, we were sitting down to our first warm, cooked meal in a few days, and I can tell you, plain rice and noodles with a touch of salt has never tasted so good! After our little feast, we quickly headed back to base camp because at that point we weren't sure whether or not we had crossed into North Korean territory. We were so energized by our victory that we decided the time had come to make our way up the mountain to get the coveted view of the famous Tianchi Crater Lake. We were so full of pent-up energy from being cooped up in our tent for three days that we ran up to the summit, where we were greeted with our first view of the "Heavenly Lake." We sat in awed silence for several minutes, taking in the view, breathing deeply and reveling in our achievement. It was another great example of Ben Hei Hei's wisdom from *Pirkei Avot*, "According to the effort, so is the reward." The more effort something takes, the more rewarding the result is. As the sun began to set, we made our way back down to our campsite, and arrived just in time as the clouds started moving in and the rain showers spread their way across the mountain once more.

The next morning, we packed up our stuff and headed out toward civilization. After treating ourselves to the first hearty meal we'd had for a few days, we made our way back to Beijing, from where we embarked on our next mega adventure: the six-day Trans-Siberian Express train journey, which cut briefly through Mongolia and then across the whole of Russia to its final destination in Moscow. From there, I traveled overland through Latvia, Estonia, and Holland, before heading back to England to see my family. I ended up staying and working in London for three months, reconnecting with friends, family, and Western civilization. Yet all that time I was planning my next adventure: to fulfill my lifelong dream of visiting the "Crown of the World," the Nepalese Himalayas.

CHAPTER 8

Nepal

Himalayas at Last

Since the age of eight, when I first laid my hands on the Willard Price Adventure books, I have been passionately enraptured by stories of survival and adventure. Among my favorite reads are two books by Jon Krakauer, *Into the Wild* and *Into Thin Air*, which tell of true survival adventures with tragic outcomes, and *The Long Walk*, by Slavomir Rawicz, which details the "true story" of a Polish prisoner of war who escaped from a Russian camp in Siberia and made an epic 6,500-kilometer journey on foot through the Gobi Desert, Tibet, and the Himalayas until finally reaching India in the winter of 1942. It was only much later that I found out that the story probably isn't true, but it was certainly enough to light a fire for adventure in my heart.

The Himalayas in particular have always fascinated me—mystically, geologically, and aesthetically—and I knew from the beginning of my journey that I'd be spending a decent amount of time in the Abode of Snow. At the same time, and looking back I'm not sure exactly why, I've never had a strong desire to do anything too crazy myself. Although the 1,200-kilometer solo hike around a Japanese island was pretty challenging,[1] it was never really life-threatening, and I was always within a few hours walk of civilization. The 1,125-kilometer

1 See chap. 9.

forty-day hike of the Israel National Trail,[2] including ten days walking through the desert and a midnight encounter with a wolf, had its challenges, but the trail in general was full of Israeli home hospitality and national park services. My near-death experience as the fog suddenly descended on the Triund Mountain in Northern India as I was making my way down could have ended pretty badly, but it was only touch-and-go for a few moments, and I probably could have survived one pretty miserable freezing cold night with some broken bones until someone would have found me in the morning. The six days in Changbaishan[3] were by no means a walk in the park, but ultimately were controlled enough to preclude any real disaster.

Summiting Everest was never a dream of mine, and solo expeditions to the North Pole never even crossed the radar. I'd like to imagine that it is because I felt full of wonder and alive enough to not have to risk my life doing crazy things, or maybe the adventures and travels I did have fed my thirst for nature, or maybe because I'm just too much of a mommy's boy to risk leaving her bereaved. Whatever the reason, I managed to get a taste of the wilderness and everything it has to offer without actually placing myself in too much imminent danger.

In any case, after a few months in England, I packed my bag once again, bid farewell to my family, who by now were getting used to saying goodbye (and planning their trip out to visit me), and headed out across the world, determined to dig deeper in my search for personal mastery. My warrior's journey was finally taking me to the mountains of my childhood dreams.

The Himalayan mountain range is a literally awe-inspiring expanse of snow-covered mountains, which cover eighty percent of Nepal's land mass. It is home to eight of the world's ten highest mountains, including, of course, Mount Everest, whose peak at 8,848 meters makes it the highest place on earth. Tales abound of great sages and yogis hidden

2 See chap.10.

3 Mountain on the border of China and North Korea—see chap. 7.

in the caves and forests, and many of the mountains themselves are considered sacred by the locals and adherents to the regional religions. Predominantly a Hindu country, Nepal also has a strong current of Buddhism running through all aspects of society, not least of all because Siddartha Gautama, the Buddha himself, was born there. The capital, Kathmandu, is a thriving, sprawling metropolis of over 1.4 million people, and while there are more modern buildings cropping up all the time, the colorful skyline is still generally taken up with traditional wooden and mud housing and stores, temples on almost every corner, and street markets selling all kinds of exotic food and other necessities. The conspicuous five-colored prayer flags that pop up all over Northern India, Nepal, and Tibet flap in the wind, and the hustle and bustle of merchants and tourists making their way through the narrow streets of this ancient city, along with cows and chickens roaming free, means it's easy to imagine what it must have been like five hundred years ago as a hodgepodge of cultures and traditions converged on this important trade center on the merchant routes between India, Tibet, and China.

I arrived there on November 9, 2004, and immediately settled back into my backpacker mindset: no pressures, no worries, just curious and free to wander wherever I chose, the sparkle of life on the trail back in my eyes. After two days of acclimatizing, exploring, and learning some Nepali, I set off on the seven-hour bus journey to Pokhara. The fact that it takes seven hours to travel the 210 kilometers between the cities gives a good impression of what the terrain and roads are like in this part of the world. Set on a large lake, framed by the awesome Annapurna Massif,[4] Pokhara is a picture-perfect gateway to some of the world's most stunning yet manageable treks, totally geared to the backpacker and trekking scene, making it Nepal's most popular tourist destination and a great place to experience mountain life.

Having settled into a guesthouse on the shores of the lake, two Americans who I met on the bus and I booked a ten-day hike up to Annapurna Base Camp, a route that took us up through barren, desert-like landscapes,

4 Mountain range.

beyond that through the forested lower slopes, and finally breaking through to the postcard-perfect vistas of the Himalayas that I'd always dreamed about. Annapurna itself is the most dangerous of the world's fourteen over-eight-thousand-meter peaks, with thirty-four percent of summit attempters not making it back down. We spent our days walking through charming villages, with farm animals crossing our path (or, more accurately, we crossing theirs); lush greenery all around; quaint cobbled streets and colorful mud houses; kids in their school uniforms playing football, using rolled-up clothes as a ball; ladders made of tree trunks with grooves cut up their length; and the constant smell of burning wood, used for cooking food and heating water for bucket showers. In the evenings, the foreign trekkers would gather in guesthouses, exchange their hiking boots (or sneakers in my case) for sandals to give the blisters some rest from rubbing, and sit with cold beers or warm teas in hand, sharing stories of their travels, playing cards, and "feasting" on *dahl baht*, the staple Nepali food of lentils and rice, or Pot Noodles and Western chocolate bars that had been schlepped up from Pokhara to bring some "luxury" to the trail. The attitude of the locals, and hence most of the trekkers, toward the mountains was one of utmost reverence and respect. Arrogance was out of place here; no one "conquered" the mountains. They were here long before us and will be around long after we depart from our temporary abode.

One evening, around four days into the trek, with still another full day of hiking to reach base camp at 4,130 meters, I was sitting on the guesthouse roof in the middle of the night, breathing the crisp thin air, the silhouette of Machupuchare[5] sharply lined against the dark-blue sky, closer to the stars than I had ever been while still on the earth, the only sound a gentle breeze wisping down the valley. I smiled as I realized that just one week ago I couldn't have been further—physically or mentally—from where I was now. Back then I was surrounded by traffic and TVs, coffee shops and clubs, celebrity gossip, creature comforts, designer clothes, fast-paced work life, sports mania, in a city with nearly six thousand people per square kilometer, all running around on the treadmill of

---

5 Fishtail Mountain, considered so sacred by the locals that no one has ever been allowed to attempt to summit it, and which is now off limits to all climbers.

life. And here I was, sitting thousands of meters above the clamor of the "real world," with no way to be contacted or to contact anyone, no technology, a small bag with a few essentials in it, nowhere to go, nothing to do apart from revel in the magical wonder of having finally made it into the mountains that had been enticing me all these years, totally serene, alone and present, feeling, in many ways, on top of the world.

ויאמר ה׳ אל משה עלה אלי ההרה והיה שם:

> *Hashem said to Moshe, "Come up to Me to the mountain, and just be there."*[6]

The term "mindfulness" is trending nowadays, with mindfulness books selling millions of copies, yoga centers popping up left and right, meditation apps flooding the market, all turning the whole "show" into a multibillion-dollar industry. Of course, this is hardly surprising given the opposite trend it's coming to balance out. According to a recent survey, the average American spends ninety percent of their waking hours looking at a screen! Most groups I speak to admit that the first thing they do when they wake up and the last thing they do before they sleep is check their phones for messages and updates. Many people work in front of a computer, watch TV at home, spend time on social media and Skype on their laptops, and constantly check their smartphones throughout the day, wherever they are. Even the gym is not immune to screens, and many people go to the movies or sports bars on their night off.

One survey I read reported that people compulsively check their email seventy-four times a day and look at their phone over one hundred and fifty times a day. The average person has at least five notification channels—WhatsApp, SMS, Facebook, phone, and email—buzzing and beeping all the time. Add to that LinkedIn, Snapchat, and Instagram—we're being constantly bombarded by technology and social media, vying

---

6 *Shemot, Parashat Mishpatim* 24:12. Heard as a source for just being in the moment, from Rav Moshe Weinberger in the name of the Modshitzer Rebbe.

relentlessly for our attention. What this means is that we are very rarely, if ever, actually alone. In fact, the thought of having no distractions and just being alone with oneself really freaks most people out.

When I tell groups that I spent ten days in silence with no reading, writing, phone, or TV, they can't believe it or understand how that's even possible. People feel the need to escape the pressures of life and the endless chatter of the mind, and when not at work, many people spend their free time actively trying to escape rather than just sitting quietly and being comfortable with their own company. TV, video games, and different forms of social media browsing make up four of the top five pastimes in America today. Some of the highest-paid people in society are the entertainers, such as sports people, and music and movie stars—people who help others tune out of their lives and take a break from their own minds for a little while.

The problem with this method is that when the temporary break from life and mind chatter comes to end, when the final whistle blows, the drugs wear off, or the credits start rolling, we're just back where we started. This can all lead to a rather meaningless and superficial relationship with ourselves, others, and life in general, as people look to get the best selfie to share on Instagram rather than actually being present and enjoying the moment.[7] Depth in life can only come from being truly present and engaged, and meaning in life can only come from being present and engaged in meaningful things, that is, things that actually lead us toward the goal and purpose of life.

Many people spend their free time actively trying to escape rather than just sitting quietly and being comfortable with their own company.

Although the mind itself is always in the past or future—planning, worrying, reminiscing, comparing, and judging—reality itself is only ever in this very present moment. Our existence is just a whole chain of present moments, influenced by the

7 My theory is (and I'd love someone to design this research) that if someone in reality liked place A more than place B, but the photos of place B got more "likes" and comments, later on they will "remember" liking place B more than place A.

past, building to the future, yet lived only now. Therefore, if we aren't being present, we are missing out on fully experiencing our lives and relating to those around us. How many parents interrupt telling their kids a bedtime story to answer their phone? What message does that send to the kids?[8]

How many people have conversations where they are just waiting for the other person to stop talking so they can share what they think and how they feel? How often do we do one thing, while thinking about something else entirely?

Like most other spiritual paths, Judaism is very focused on bringing its practitioners consciously into the present moment. Jewish practice emphasizes the value of stopping and becoming aware of where you are, what you are doing, and why you are doing it.

There are two main parts to mindfulness: awareness and intention.

Awareness means becoming highly conscious of what is happening in the present moment, externally and internally, without judgments or comparisons. It means being centered and present, not just going through the motions. If we were truly aware of what we were doing, we'd never leave the house and forget if we'd locked the door or turned off the oven, we'd never have a doubt whether we'd made an after-*berachah* or not, and we wouldn't let unwanted negative thoughts keep going through our minds.

Jewish practice emphasizes the value of stopping and becoming aware of where you are, what you are doing, and why you are doing it.

In Jewish practice there are many things we say and do to promote this awareness. For example, there is a phrase we say before each mitzvah we do, which begins:

הנני מוכן ומזומן לקיים מצוות עשה של...

Behold, I am prepared and ready to perform the mitzvah of…

---

8 I used to turn off my phone when I read my kids stories in bed at night. Now I leave the phone on, but a little quieter, so when it rings and my kids say, "Abba, your phone is ringing," I can say, "I know, but what's more important, the phone or you?" before carrying on reading.

This brings us into the moment and focuses us on what we are about to do. All mitzvot themselves are physical acts, such as lighting candles, shaking a lulav and etrog, tefillin, and tzedakah, which give us an anchor in the present moment in the physical world. Yet they are much more than just that.

A remarkable distinction I have found in Jewish mindfulness is the reality that not only do we need to tap into the present moment, but that there are specific present moments in which there is a different energy or spiritual reality we need to become aware of. Our Sages teach us that at different times of the day, week, month, and year, there are different energies being "pumped into" Creation, energies that can only be tapped into by doing specific acts. For example, the energy present in Creation just before sundown on Friday night is very different from that of an hour after nightfall on Pesach. As the sun sets on Friday night, the present moment calls for lighting candles; on Pesach night, we need to eat matzah. A Jew sitting in a temple in the Himalayas meditating and gazing at the moon on the fifteenth of Nissan can be very present to feelings and thoughts and sensations, can feel very blissful and connected to his soul and all of existence, yet the Torah teaches that if he isn't eating matzah, he isn't tapping into the intrinsic Divine energy and nature of that moment. It doesn't mean he is a bad person—indeed, theoretically, he may be much nicer and friendlier and more spiritual than someone eating matzah in Jerusalem. It's just that he's missing a huge opportunity to be connected to Hashem in the highest way.

Our Sages teach that our forefathers fulfilled the mitzvot long before the Torah was given; for example, Avraham ate matzah on Pesach! Now we can understand how this is possible. They were so spiritually in tune that they could feel the energy in Creation at that time and knew the appropriate action to connect to it. They didn't fast on Yom Kippur because they were told to, it's just that they couldn't possibly bring themselves to eat that day because they were too busy doing *teshuvah* (repentance). They didn't fast on Tishah b'Av because the Temple was destroyed (it hadn't even been built yet), they just couldn't eat because they were grieving over all the negativity in the world.[9] Those of us who aren't as spiritually in tune need the Guidebook to let us know what needs to be done at each moment, and to help us to tune in to reality.

The second part of mindfulness is **intention**: being conscious of why you are doing something (your motivating factor) and what you hope to achieve. The above phrase that is said before doing a mitzvah often continues with "לעשות נחת רוח ליוצרנו—to give *nachat* to our Creator." Although the word *nachat* is colloquially translated as pride or a pleasant feeling, the phrase literally means the "landing of the spirit," i.e., bringing Divine consciousness and presence into this act. It could also be read as "to settle my own spirit down and focus it toward the Creator." This phrase therefore serves to fully tune us into what we are doing and why we're doing it.

One major idea we see from this is that in Judaism, mindfulness is by no means the end goal. Mindfulness of the present moment—observing and accepting what is—is important and feels great and blissful. Tapping into the "Power of Now"[10] is a fundamental tool we need in our lives to help us find peace and personal empowerment. However, it is only a means to an end, a tool to assist us in achieving the real purpose, which is expressed in perhaps the key verse in the Torah:[11]

> ועתה ישראל מה ה' אלקיך שואל מעמך כי אם ליראה את ה' אלקיך:
>
> *Now, Yisrael, what does Hashem ask of you,* ***only this****: to have* יראה*—yirah!*[12]

יראה, often translated as awe, comes from the word רואה, to see. The Torah is urging us to work on becoming G-d-conscious, to find and see Godliness in a world in which Divinity is so hidden. With a physical body, negative traits and mind patterns, pressures from life, and no obvious revelation of

---

9 The Talmud (*Yoma* 28b) teaches that Rav holds that Avraham kept the whole Torah, and Raba (or Rabbi Ashi) extends this and holds that Avraham kept even Rabbinic decrees.

10 See chap. 6.

11 *Devarim* 10:12.

12 The verse continues and lists four other qualities that are either things in their own right (*Mesilat Yesharim*) or are things that come through having *yirah* (*Imrei Emet*).

Hashem in the world, the task of connecting in an authentic way is extremely challenging. Yet this challenge is the whole point of our time in this world: we are to work for and earn the connection when it is not so apparent.[13]

Just being blissfully mindful, without having a relationship with Hashem, feels great—but it's missing the whole point.

Just being blissfully mindful, without having a relationship with Hashem, feels great—but it's missing the whole point.

One of the key tools to bring this awareness into everyday life, which is actually learned from the same verse in the Torah,[14] is the recital of one hundred blessings a day. If said with consciousness and intention, it means one hundred mini-connection points to the present moment spread throughout the day, every day! Everything we eat, every mitzvah we perform, even every time we go to the bathroom, we have a moment of mindfulness and appreciation as we say a blessing and connect to what we are doing and why we are doing it. The word *baruch* can mean "the source of all blessing,"[15] "an increase in something,"[16] and it can also mean to "lower down."[17] This implies that every time we say *baruch*, we are "pulling down" G-d-consciousness into the world, thereby standing "face-to-face" with Hashem, at which point we can truly address Hashem as "*Atah*—You," demonstrating our intimate relationship with a G-d who is immanently present in our lives.

Mindfulness of eating plays itself out through the laws of *kashrut*: what we can and can't eat, waiting between meat and milk, saying *berachot*, and eating special foods for different occasions. The laws of modesty help us be mindful of which images we let enter our consciousness, how we project ourselves to and interact with other people,

---

13 For further reading, see the idea of "*nehama d'kisufa*—the bread of shame" for example, see Chaim Vital, *Likutei Torah* (Vilna: 1879), *Haazinu*, p. 108a.

14 *Menachot* 43b: "Rabbi Meir said: A person is obligated to bless one hundred blessing every day, as the Torah says, 'Now Israel, what does God ask from you, but only to have awe of Hashem your God...' (Deut. 10:12,13). Don't read *mah*—what, read *me'ah*—one hundred."

15 See the Responsa of the Rashba 5:51.

16 For example, see Rashi, *Vayikra* 26:5 on ואכלתם לחמכם לשבע.

17 See *Bereishit* 24:11. See Rashi, who says Eliezer made the camels lie down.

including our spouses, making sure it is in a respectful and healthy way. Mindfulness of time is expressed through Shabbat and holidays, on which we get to unplug, turn off the screens and notifications, and reconnect to ourselves and our loved ones. Prayer services give us these little islands in time every day—morning, afternoon, and night—helping us realign our focus and values.[18] Of course, even prayer and *berachot* can be superficial and meaningless if the ancient Hebrew words are just mumbled with no thought, just an obligation we have to get out the way before we can get back to things we deem more important. A person can learn Torah, pray, and say blessings all day, yet completely miss the point of life if he does it unconsciously and without intention and joy. In fact, G-d himself said that He is not interested in mitzvot done this way.[19] The Divine system is there, set up to give us constant reminders to reconnect to the present moment and tap into the purpose of life; it's our job to interact with it and implement the tools in the right way.

The Baal Shem Tov taught that the greatest obstacle to real spiritual growth and connection is doing things habitually. He learns this from the first meeting of Hashem and Moshe Rabbeinu.[20] Hashem says to Moshe, "של נעליך מעל רגליך—Take off your shoes from on your feet." The second half of the verse seems rather redundant; Moshe knew where his shoes were! The Baal Shem Tov teaches that the root of the word for shoes, נעליך, has the meaning "to lock," while the root of רגליך, feet, is "הרגל—habit." He teaches that Hashem is saying that to have an authentic relationship with Him, Moshe will have to unlock his habits, do things fresh and new every time.

We see this idea every week at *Kabbalat Shabbat* when we sing, " שירו לה' שיר חדש— Sing to Hashem a new song."[21] The truth is that it's not new at all! We sang it last week, and the week before, and the week before that, and David HaMelech wrote it three thousand years ago!

18 According to Jewish law, one shouldn't do anything before praying in the morning apart from those things that prepare you for prayer. This means that by the time you've gotten up, washed your hands, gotten dressed, and prayed, it's at least an hour and a half before you can even check your phone!

19 See *Yeshayahu* 1:13.

20 *Shemot* 3:5.

21 *Tehillim* 96.

The point is that we need to approach the song with newness each week because we have grown and become new people—we can therefore see it from a new perspective. It's not the same me or the same moment as it was last week. When people ask me how they can do the same thing every day without it becoming stale or habitual, I ask in return if they ever get tired of telling their children how much they love them. Once you truly value something and love it, it never gets old.

Try these Enlightened Jewish Master mindfulness practices.

- **Make time to be alone.** Most people do whatever they can to not be alone—without a phone, book, or newspaper. We don't like being alone because our minds run wild, and we want to distract ourselves. Rav Itamar Schwartz teaches that the power to be alone is deep within us and is a vital need for the *neshamah*.[22] Adam was created alone, the world was silent when the Torah was given, and many of the forefathers were shepherds, which enabled them to spend time alone. Take five minutes to just sit and be. There should be no distractions; your phone in particular should be far from you. Just breathe deeply and appreciate being alive. Get used to spending time with yourself without running away. You'll find that you're actually pretty great company.
- **Before saying a *berachah***, think three things:
    1. What am I about to say? (Do I understand the words and meaning of the *berachah*?)
    2. Who am I saying it to? (Am I actually speaking directly to Hashem, or am I just mumbling some words to myself or the food?)

22 *Getting to Know Yourself* (Bilvavi Books, 2011), part 1, chap. 3. The ultimate goal is not to be alone, but we need to be able to be alone—and when we are, we can then be much more present for other people. For more on this check out my class at www.soundcloud.com/dov-ber-cohen/getting-to-know-yourself-part-seven.

3. How am I going to say it? (Joyfully and consciously, or resentfully and unthinkingly?)

- **When saying the *berachah*,** pause for a few seconds on either the word "אתה—You," or after saying Hashem's Name. Breathe deeply and try to actually feel the Presence of Hashem (I often say in my head, "Hashem, I'm actually speaking to You now") and then finish off the *berachah*. That will make several times a day of consciously connecting to ourselves and G-d in a joyful, appreciative way.
- **Before saying or doing something**, ask yourself: Would a *tzaddik* say or do this? If not, don't do it. Note down every time you succeed.
- **Whenever you arrive in a new place**, take time to just look, observe, listen, and smell. Notice how you are feeling—take it all in. You can do this anywhere, just stop for a few moments and observe everything.
- **Think to yourself** that this could be the last time you get to do or see this thing.[23] Before *Minchah*, think that this could be your last *Minchah*. When you walk past a tree on your way to work, take time to stop and look at it—start finding wonder in simple things.
- **Limit your time on the phone.** Set certain hours, or a certain number of times a day you can check. Never bring the phone into shul or the *beit midrash*.
- **List some bad habits**, for example, slouching, biting nails, or compulsively checking your phone. Once you have listed them you'll become more aware of them. When you notice yourself doing them, smile and correct them.

By putting these things into practice, you'll soon find that following the Torah in a conscious and joyful way leads to a meaningful and

23 This is based on *Chovot HaLevavot, Shaar Cheshbon HaNefesh*. Don't try this consciousness tool if it will make you afraid or morbid.

mindful life in which it is possible to build an authentic relationship with and connection to the Ever Present One—the One Who is always in the present moment.

David HaMelech entreats us in *Tehillim* to "טעמו וראו כי טוב ה'—taste and see that Hashem is good."[24] We all know that taste is something that can't be described (try telling someone who's never tasted a strawberry what strawberries taste like). It can only be a personal experience in the present moment. We need to have an intimate experience of Hashem, not just learn, think, and talk about Him. In fact, the *Tikunei Zohar* teaches that "לית מחשבה תפיסא ביה כלל—no thought can grasp Hashem's essence at all."[25] Therefore, it appears that the spiritual work of being able to taste (i.e., experience) Hashem comes from going beyond compulsive overthinking, which is always in the past or future, and coming into the present moment, where we can connect deeply and authentically with the Source of our being.

I believe that it was with this in mind that last summer, while running a four-day silent-meditation retreat in the countryside just outside of Jerusalem, I was contemplating Jewish mindfulness and the famous words of the *Tikunei Zohar* above. We had been studying the idea of No Mind or No Thought, a state in which the mind's consistent chatter has died down and the practitioner gets to experience the peace that lies behind all the noise. It suddenly occurred to me that the phrase from the *Zohar* could be read with slightly different punctuation, to beautifully and clearly express the idea that an experience of Hashem can only really come from beyond thought. I picked up my pen and with a big smile jotted down in my notebook my first ever Zen poem:

24 34:9.

25 *Tikunei Zohar* 121:2.

Leit Machshavah—No thought[26]
Tfisa Bei—Grasps Him!
Klal—That's a rule.[27]

Gazing across Phewa Lake, I could see the pure white pagoda perched on the top of Ananda Hill, brightly reflecting the afternoon sun, beckoning me to make the pilgrimage to meditate in its surrounding gardens. The Shanti Stupa is one of eighty such structures set up by a Japanese monk after being inspired by his meeting with Gandhi in 1931 to spread peace and love throughout the world. It had been two days since my return from my Annapurna Base Camp trek, and it was time for a new adventure, time to separate myself from the tourist hub that made up the one side of the lake and get over to the other side, where people would only tend to visit on day trips. By this time, my Nepalese was pretty good so I knew I could make a go of it. There were locals waiting on the banks of the lake, offering boat rides to the famous Tal Barahi Temple on an island in the middle of the lake, or across to the stupa on the other side. After a bit of bargaining, including a couple of Nepali folk songs to lighten the mood, I persuaded one of the men to lend me his boat so I could row myself to the opposite shore, where I'd leave it for him to pick up next time his cousin went across. I set off and, having hit the center of the lake, decided to pull in the oars and lie back to appreciate the clear blue sky for a while and relish the freedom of being completely alone once again. As dusk started to fall, I decided to make my way to the other shore, and as the day visitors were beginning to return, I felt the feeling of triumph once again as I rowed against the stream, off to another unknown destination and the adventures it promised.

We need to have an intimate experience of Hashem, not just learn, think, and talk about Him.

26 A state beyond thought in which the mind is quiet.
27 *Klal* can mean "at all" or "a rule."

I parked the boat on the shore and started making my way up the steep hill that lay behind the thin beach, not sure what I'd find. In a clearing halfway up the hill, I was greeted by Binod, a young Nepali guy with a huge smile, clearly delighted for the company and hopeful for the business. He had a ramshackle two-room "guesthouse" that had clearly seen better days. As it was already getting dark, I decided to stay for the night and make my way up to the stupa the next morning. We lit a fire and cooked some *dahl baht*, which we ate while sitting on his roof, playing the bamboo flute and singing folk songs until the heavens were lit up by the myriad stars of the Himalayan night sky.

One day turned into two, two into three, and in the end, Binod's little guesthouse became my home for just under two marvelous weeks. Every morning, I'd rise before the sun and make my way up to the deserted stupa, silhouetted against the dawn sky. I became friendly with Durega, the caretaker, a simple man from the village who always wore a bright orange tracksuit top, white shorts, and sandals and who was valiantly trying to wean himself of his alcohol dependence. We'd sit inside for a while banging the large taiko drums, repeating a mantra over and over again as the sun rose over the mountains, painting the sky an awesome mixture of oranges, reds, and light pink, before the first tourists started to trickle in. My days were spent between the stupa and Binod's guesthouse, where I ended up helping out, greeting and making lunch for travelers on their way up to the pagoda, and even getting some of them to take the other room that I wasn't using. During the day, I'd help schlep bricks up the hill to build a small meditation cell, and then go off to find a quiet spot to focus on my breath and rise beyond the confines of the physical world. One day, I had the privilege of going to a wedding in a nearby village, where I met Binod's family and managed to make excuses as to why I couldn't marry his fourteen-year-old sister. In the early evening, I'd go back up to the stupa and help Durega tidy up after the tourists had left, have a final meditation session of the day, before making my way home, where Durega, Binod, and I, and occasionally a traveler who stayed the night, would cook up some dinner, crack open some beers, and chat and sing the night away.

At the time, those twelve days felt like some of the most wonderful of my life. Sitting on a patch of grass, the grandeur of the Annapurna Massif as a backdrop, clear blue skies, no sounds apart from the birds singing and the breeze rustling the leaves on the trees, no company apart from the eagles flying overhead and the ants and beetles scurrying past, just a book, a piece of fruit, and some water in my backpack, no responsibilities, no one needing my attention, able to just tap into the peace of the present moment. It was truly blissful, and at the time I felt no lack.

Yet many years later, sitting alone in the Jerusalem forest, clear blue skies, no sounds apart from the birds singing and the breeze rustling the leaves on the trees, no company apart from the birds flying overhead, the ants and beetles scurrying past, just a book, a piece of fruit, and some water in my backpack, that present, clear, empty space that I felt in Nepal was now present, clear, and *full*, saturated with an authentic personal connection to the Divine Creator of all things, as I was beginning to taste and see the goodness of Hashem.

CHAPTER 9

Japan

Forty-Day Pilgrimage and Aikido Training

"Come—attack me however you like."

This is the proposition my aikido sensei issued to me on my first day in his dojo.

I already had a black belt in taekwondo and had trained in shaolin, so I was a little hesitant to attack this gentle and dignified older Japanese man.

"Come on then, what are you waiting for?"

Cautiously, I moved toward him, and before I knew it, I was on the floor with my arm pinned behind my back, face squashed against the training mats.

"While you are here, you can attack me whenever you want; in the changing room, on the street, if you see me in a restaurant—just go for it."

There was no challenge or arrogance in his voice at all. It was very matter-of-fact. In fact, he said it quite lovingly, as if he were offering to treat me to dinner.

It took me less than a week to realize that it was not a good idea to take him up on his kind offer; rather, the first lesson I learned was to humble myself at the feet of a true master...

In writing this book, no other place has brought up such a deep nostalgia in my mind and fondness in my heart as has Japan. Nowhere was I happier and more fulfilled than I was during my fifteen-month stay in Tanabe, a small town on the southern coast of Honshu, the biggest of Japan's four main islands. The strikingly diverse natural landscapes, where the shoguns and ninjas once roamed, the society still permeated with Zen Buddhist mindfulness, samurai stoicism, Shinto-based spirit and animistic beliefs, the pristine beaches, colorful temples, ancient shrines, and remote hiking trails through the mountains, all mixed in with modern efficiency, technology, and cleanliness make Japan a truly magical place to live. Tanabe is sandwiched (or should I say, "sushied") between an immaculate white sand beach and mystical rolling hills dotted with Shinto shrines, waterfalls, and *onsen* (natural hot springs). The small town is the entranceway to the Kumano Kodo, a sacred pilgrimage trail that makes its way from one coast to the other across Japan's largest peninsula, stopping at three of Japan's holiest shrines on the way. Tanabe, like most places in Japan, has several magnificent local *matsuri* (festivals) in which the whole town comes out to parade colorful costumes, playing traditional music and performing folk dances through the streets. It is home of the *ume boshi*, the world-famous pickled plum, whose power was said to be so great that a samurai could walk for a whole day on just one of these small delicacies. I was enamored with Japanese culture, from my apartment with its traditional matted tatami flooring and shoji (sliding paper doors), to intricate and refined traditional customs such as chanoyu (the tea ceremony) and ikebana (flower arranging), both inspired by Zen mindfulness meditations. From enthralling tales of heroic samurai warriors and their martial art and survival feats, to the amazing variety of regional cuisine, Japan was truly a feast for the senses.

I had a wonderful group of local friends, the youngest of whom was about sixty-five years old, with whom I played tennis, went hiking, soaked in *onsens*, and had lavish meals spiced up with warm sake (rice wine). I loved my work teaching English in an after-school academy to Japanese people of all ages, and the other gaijin (foreigners) in town were great to hang out with. I had Japanese lessons, sang traditional Japanese songs in the karaoke bars, trained in aikido, played the piano in classy (and not-so-classy) jazz bars, and was gifted a large Suzuki motorbike by a teacher who was leaving and couldn't sell it. I used to ride off into the mountains for solo hiking expeditions, scrambling over rock formations and along streams and emerging at the top to be greeted with panoramic sunset views of Tanabe and the coastline stretching out as far as the eye could see in both directions.

Tanabe is also the birthplace, home, and resting place of Ueshiba Morihei, founder of modern aikido and according to some, "the greatest martial artist to ever have lived." The dignified and honorable art of aikido seemed appropriate to study there, and my many hours of meditation in the mountains and next to the grave of O Sensei (the Great Teacher) helped me tap into the pulse of the town, the culture, the history, and aikido itself—the Way of the Harmonious Spirit.

> *I suddenly forgot all the martial techniques I had ever learned. The techniques of my teachers appeared completely new. Now they were vehicles for the cultivation of life, knowledge, and virtue, not devices to throw people with.*
>
> *Ueshiba Morihei*

Beyond just a defense and fighting system, martial arts in the East were fused with spirituality and religious ideals, becoming a way of life and a path to self-perfection. Practitioners focused on what is the appropriate action and reaction in any given situation—physical, emotional, mental, and spiritual. They delved into meditation and mindfulness, discipline and focus, morality and healing, connection to the Tao[1] energy of the universe, and going with the flow of life.

I'd like to say that I was on the level to embody this spirit of martial arts in my training, but because I was a little overexcitable and immature (one

1 The Tao can be loosely defined as the flow of the universe, or as some essence or pattern behind the natural world that keeps the universe balanced and ordered (Wikipedia).

master said to me, "You know, you don't need to make those silly noises..." referring to my Bruce Lee-esque shrieking), and I was getting that spirituality from meditation in nature, my martial arts was mainly about physical training, fighting styles, and energy release. I completely reveled in the hours of intense training, practicing the same foot movements, blocks, stretches, kicks, punches, and forms thousands of times. Although I was never very flexible, I had one main asset: my energy. Hold up pads for me and I could keep kicking them all day, spar with me and you'd have to knock me out to stop me coming at you. I had to punch out candles without touching them, jump onto walls and rebound into a kick with the same foot to break wooden boards, jump through hoops and over chairs, and chop through the boards with the tips of my fingers in knife hand form.

Added to that was all the weight and stamina training—hours in the gym, early morning runs along the beach or up the surrounding hills, and excruciating stretching routines to open up my hips for those good ol' spinning roundhouse kicks. I relished every day of it as I reflected on the fact that I was actually living my own real-life Kickboxer/Rocky IV training scene.[2]

The one thing that really stood out in training was the immense attention to detail. My masters worked on how I was standing, breathing, moving, the angle of my fist, the way I looked at my adversary, what I could eat, and even what I was thinking. To be a black belt, to avoid getting knocked out, to be able to act and react in the highest way possible, takes precision, attention to detail, and lots of practice.

To be a black belt, to avoid getting knocked out, to be able to act and react in the highest way possible, takes precision, attention to detail, and lots of practice.

This turned out to be a huge insight for me as I was starting to connect to my Jewish roots. One of my biggest challenges with Judaism was all the seemingly superfluous little details. Wash your hands like this, eat exactly this amount of bread, don't use the same plate for milk and meat, can't say this,

2 The films with arguably the best training scenes.

can't do that. At the time, it seemed to me that Jews were caught up the whole time in meaningless rituals made up by a group of men who didn't have anything better to do than make life unbearably dull and difficult, whereas Buddhism was about presence, inner peace, enlightenment, and other such universal and expansive ideas. I thought to myself, "If G-d is the infinite, loving Divine Creator of all reality, why on earth (or heaven) does He (or She) care if I tear toilet paper on Saturday? Surely He should be spending His time sorting out war and famine, not caring if I put my right shoe on first or stick a small box on the doorposts of my house."

Then one day it hit me.

In all areas of life, when we value something, details count. The sports fans who watch the video replay to see if the ball was half a centimeter over the line or not, the CEO running his business, the heart surgeon doing her work, the husband making his wife her tea just how she likes it—attention to detail gives life its depth and meaning, it's what creates real connection and personal mastery. Far from Hashem being an angry dictator in the sky and the Torah being His book of laws for me to follow (or else!), I started to see Hashem as the ultimate martial arts Master, and Jewish laws as the tools guiding me toward living the most conscious, moral, and intentional life possible. I realized that by mindfully following the system of halachah (Jewish law), I would get to live fully and meaningfully, connecting to the present moment, raising my level of consciousness, and moving through life with the appropriate thoughts, speech, actions, and reactions in all situations—in other words, being a true martial artist in the way Ueshiba himself defined it. The *Zohar*[3] teaches that the 613 mitzvot are actually pieces of advice guiding us toward self-realization, and the word halachah comes from the root "to walk," meaning that halachah teaches us how to walk through life consciously and intentionally.

Take putting your shoes on, for example. The law says that you must put your right shoe on first, then your left.[4] Seems a bit pointless, until you realize that it means you have to take a second to stop and be present

3 2.82b.

4 *Shulchan Aruch* 2:4.

in the moment as you choose which shoe to put on. Then, learning a little deeper, we understand that right represents *chessed*, loving-kindness. We want to start our day with loving-kindness, bringing it into our lives and making sure we interact with others in this way throughout the day. (The bride and groom both step under the *chuppah* with their right foot first, symbolizing their intention to build a home based on *chessed.*) We learn that left represents *gevurah*, meaning strength and boundaries, as we sometimes need to rein in the unconditional love so as not to overwhelm others or be taken advantage of. If I put on my left shoe first, G-d isn't going to freak out and punish me. It just means I lost an opportunity to have a conscious connection to the present moment, to turn a mundane act into something meaningful and holy. This goes for all actions throughout the day—how we wash our hands, talk to people, go to bed, wake up, go to the bathroom, walk—each act during the day is a portal and a connection point to higher consciousness.

Once, as I was becoming more observant, one of my friends said to me, "You're so unlucky. You used to be so free, now you have to make a *berachah* before you eat anything and you have to follow all these laws—don't you feel so restricted?" I explained that I don't **have to** make a *berachah*, I **get to** make a *berachah*. It's an amazing opportunity to uplift eating to a holy practice beyond just the physical act itself. Then (speaking in the best Bruce Lee voice I could muster), I explained:

> *Freedom is not defined as having no rules. Just eating whatever you like, smoking whatever you like, doing whatever you want does not mean you are free. It just means you are a slave to your desires, moods, ego, conditioning, and what your society expects of you. True freedom comes from understanding the point of the game and mastering the laws so you can fully express yourself and move toward the goal.*

Someone who wants to express themselves fully through art needs to be familiar with the laws of shading, tone, perspective, and depth. A great composer needs to understand pitch, harmony, and what each instrument adds to a melody. Chefs need to know how much of which spice, how long it should cook for, which wines go with which food. And in martial arts, if you don't know the rules and forms, you're going to get knocked out. Why should spirituality and personal mastery be any different?

The word Torah comes from the root הוראה , instructions, teaching us that the Torah is an instruction manual for living the most powerful, meaningful, conscious, moral, conscientious, joyful, connected life possible.

I used to believe that becoming more observant and following the rules meant giving up my Self for what the rabbis and G-d told me to do and be. Yet I found that, to the contrary, it meant finally becoming free to fully express myself beyond my society, conditioning, and desires. *Pirkei Avot*[5] teaches that "אין לך בן חורין אלא מי שעוסק בתלמוד תורה," you can't be called free unless you are seriously studying the Guidebook. It is impossible to underestimate the crucial role Torah learning has in our life, as we say in davening every day, "תלמוד תורה כנגד כולם—learning Torah is equal to doing all the other mitzvot." If learned in the right way, it is truly food for our soul.

Mussar helps us work on our character traits, halachah guides us how to live consciously and meaningfully, Talmud helps us refine our minds and thinking to the ultimate level, *chassidut* and Kabbalah give us the inner depth of the Torah, and *machshavah* helps us form our worldview. One of my mentors said to me that although I'm a good speaker with a powerful message, if I'm not learning Torah,[6] in the end I'm just an inspiring clown.[7] There is no way to reach true heights of Jewish enlightenment without making set times for real Torah study. *Chapping* a *daf yomi shiur* before work, or learning a bit on Shabbat afternoon is very precious and praiseworthy, yet the more time we can make for learning, the more we prioritize it in our lives, the more conscious and connected we will be.

---

5 6:2.

6 Specifically, Gemara *b'iyun* (in-depth Talmud study).

7 That really hit home, and even when I got married, finished my *semichah* program, and couldn't learn full-time anymore, I made sure to have a learning *seder* of at least four hours a day. If I'm not learning Torah, I start to feel down and disconnected. I have noticed that many *baalei teshuvah* who struggle later on are the ones who stopped serious learning—כי הם חיינו ואורך ימינו ובהם נהגה יומם ולילה.

Every Enlightened Jewish Master knows that the key to real success and sustained growth is *cheshbon ha'nefesh*, making an accounting of one's actions. There is no way to become a *tzaddik* without charting and keeping tabs on one's life. A businessman has a spreadsheet for every area of the business—finances, employees, social media, marketing, goals, etc., because he doesn't want to miss an opportunity to make money or trip up and lose any money. So too, if we are truly committed to growth, we need to set goals and evaluate our progress, eliminating bad habits and retraining ourselves toward greatness. The *Mesilat Yesharim* teaches that there is

> *...a need for a man to be meticulous and weigh his ways each and every day like the great merchants who continuously evaluate all of their business matters in order that they not degenerate. He should fix definite times and hours for this weighing so that it not be haphazard but rather with the greatest regularity, for it yields great results.*[8]

The *Chovot HaLevavot* lists thirty things we should contemplate each day,[9] and in his famous work, *Cheshbon Hanefesh*, Rabbi Mendel of Satanov lays out a comprehensive system for charting personal growth.

The truth is that life is quite simple. There are just three steps:

1. Work out what the goal is (יתברר ויתאמת אצל האדם מה חובתו בעולמו).[10]
2. Understand what steps must be taken to reach the goal (למה צריך שישים מבטו ומגמתו בכל אשר הוא עמל כל ימי חייו).[11]
3. Do them!

---

8 Chap. 3, "*Zehirut*—Vigilance": והנני רואה צורך לאדם שיהיה מדקדק ושוקל דרכיו דבר יום ביומו כסוחרים הגדולים אשר יפלסו תמיד כל עסקיהם למען לא יתקלקלו, ויקבע עתים ושעות לזה שלא יהיה משקלו עראי, אלא בקביעות גדול, כי רב התולדה הוא.

9 *Chovot HaLevavot, Shaar Cheshbon HaNefesh.*

10 *Mesilat Yesharim*, chap. 1.

11 Ibid.

With this in mind, an essential Enlightened Jewish Master training exercise is to make yourself an Excel spreadsheet (or do this in a notepad) called, "Becoming a Tzaddik—Enlightened Jewish Master."[12] One simple, practical, and achievable way of doing this is as follows:

- First, define what that means to you so you have a clear goal. (My personal definition is "One who has perfected his character traits and actions,[13] living each moment mindfully and intimately connected to Hashem, through consciously and joyously following the Guidelines of the Torah, and helping others do the same.")
- In the first column, write areas you want to work on: e.g., *waking up, berachot, Torah learning, health, relationships, davening.*
- Remember that on the one hand, the more comprehensive we are, the better chance we have of succeeding.[14] Yet we must also prioritize certain things at certain times and always take small steps to ensure we don't fall into the trap of "תפסת מרבה לא תפסת,"[15] taking on too much and thereby losing everything.
- Define what these things involve, such as *Wake-up: before 7:00 AM, Modeh Ani with kavanah, negel vasser by the bed, in a good mood. Health: ten minutes of exercise a day, ten push-ups, no pizza during the week...*
- Along the top row, write ratings, such as 1–5.
- At least once a week (but really once a day, if possible) go through the chart and rate yourself (honestly!). It could only take a few minutes. Feel inspired and uplifted by the areas

12 In fact, if you don't do this, it's very unlikely you will be able to do any of the other exercises consistently. See appendix for a sample chart.

13 Essentially, the list in *Devarim* 10:12: *yirah, la'lechet b'chol derachav, ahavah, avodah, mitzvot.*

14 The *Chovot HaLevavot* teaches, "You should know, my brother, you won't be able to be strong in all areas if you ignore one of them, as they are like pearls connected on a string. If you release even one of them, they'll all be scattered and the connection will be lost."

15 *Yoma* 80a.

you are doing well in and become aware of areas that need work and adjust your behaviour accordingly.

- It is best to have a mentor or accountability partner/growth *chavruta* to make sure you are moving ahead steadily. Give them access to your spreadsheet.

Just getting these things done is a huge victory in itself. However, the truth is that much more is being asked of us than just doing what we're meant to do. The Torah teaches[16] that bad consequences happen to us not necessarily because we fail to do mitzvot, but because we don't do them *b'simchah*, with true joy. That seems a bit extreme. After all, I'm doing what I'm meant to do (even if I don't want to do it). Yet doing a mitzvah without *simchah* is like begrudgingly buying my wife flowers because it's the right thing to do. Yes, I did what I was meant to do, but I missed the whole point of it, which was to build and nurture the deep connection between us. We need to learn to want to do—and love doing—what we're meant to do. And the truth is, on a soul level, there is nothing we want to do and love doing and that gives us true *simchah* other than mitzvot.

When *Pirkei Avot* teaches, "עשה רצונו כרצונך—Make His will your will,"[17] it really means to connect to our own deepest will, which is to do mitzvot. Whereas our body/ego self chases and gets vitality from physical and ego pleasures in the world, our *neshamah* has absolutely no interest in cheesecake and honor. Rather, it gets *simchah* and vitality only from mitzvot and doing the right thing. When the Torah urges us to "choose life,"[18] it is telling us to draw our vitality from a connection to our souls, to the Torah, and Hashem, rather than our body and ego. When we are told that the Books of Life and Death are open on Rosh Hashanah, it means spiritual life and death, as the *pasuk*[19] says, "ואתם הדבקים בה' אלקיכם חיים כלכם היום—Those who feel their intimate connection with Hashem

---

16 *Devarim* 28:47, *Parashat Ki Tavo*.

17 *Pirkei Avot* 2:4.

18 *Devarim* 30:19, *Parashat Nitzavim*.

19 Ibid., 4:4, *Parashat Va'etchanan*.

are truly alive today." (Those who don't are not really called alive.) The sheer pleasure a *tzaddik* gets from putting on tefillin is infinitely greater than any amount of physical and ego pleasure we could have. The Arizal said he reached his high spiritual level not (only) from prayer, Torah learning, and meditation, but rather from *simchah shel mitzvah*, the joy he derived from doing mitzvot.

Baruch Hashem, I still have an extremely long way to go to becoming a *tzaddik* and mastering life, but at least I'm very clear on the goal, how to get there, and am committed to putting in the effort. This gives me a fighting chance. When I started understanding the path more deeply, integrating the knowledge and keeping track of my progress, I began performing the mitzvot more joyously and consciously. In this way I soon saw that the Torah, mitzvot, and halachot, far from being restrictive and burdensome obligations, are, in fact, the Divine keys we need to help us become real Black Belts in life.

Torah, mitzvot, and halachot, far from being restrictive and burdensome obligations, are, in fact, the Divine keys we need to help us become real Black Belts in life.

> *The journey is best experienced walked solo. It's tough, but that's when the learning and insights occur.*
>
> *Posted on the O-Henro forum*

As soon as I heard about the 1,200-kilometer circular pilgrimage around Shikoku Island to eighty-eight Buddhist temples, no amount of samurai on horseback or ninjas hiding in the roofs could stop me from giving it a go. Okay, so maybe my aikido master could have stopped me single-handedly, literally, but nonetheless I had my heart and mind set on the adventure from the moment its existence was brought to my attention. Every year, thousands of O-henro-san (pilgrims) undertake to visit each temple along the route, where, on arrival, they perform elaborate rituals, including washing hands at the gate, ringing the *bonsho* bell, offering incense and coins, visiting each of the different temple buildings on site to recite specific *goeika* (sacred poems) and *honzon* mantras, practicing meditation, and chanting the *Heart Sutra*, said by many to be the foundational teaching of Mahayana Buddhism. Set out in a 280-word treatise, I had memorized the *Heart Sutra* by the time I reached temple number seventeen and would repeat it many times over as I walked the trail, trying to focus myself on the path to satori (sudden enlightenment).

Shikoku Island is split up into four prefectures, which to the pilgrim represent different stages on the journey of life. The trail starts in Hosshin no Dojo,[20] "the Dojo of Awakening Faith," where the yearning for and belief in something beyond takes root. From there, the *henro* enters the Shugyo no Dojo, "the Dojo of Religious Discipline," where the work of transformation and spiritual cultivation takes place. The third stage is the Bodai no Dojo, "the Dojo of Awakening," where the enlightening effects of the effort start to be felt. Finally comes the Nehan no Dojo, "the Dojo of Enlightenment," where you can sit down and bask in the splendor of life. From here, the pilgrim reenters everyday life, but by now he has a whole new perspective on how to live.

Most of the *henro* are Japanese tourists who complete the route by bus or car, taking ten days to two weeks to visit each temple. Many *aruki-henro* (walking pilgrims) spread the pilgrimage out over several years, taking a week or two in the summer to walk as far as they can and then returning the next year to start up again where they left off. Then there are the few of us with more time on our hands, who set off to complete the trail by foot in one go.

As soon as my contract at the English academy came to an end, I packed my bag—a couple of pairs of shorts, a couple of T-shirts (all beige or white, to identify myself as a pilgrim), a small towel, a mosquito net, a rain poncho, a padded roll-up mat to sleep on, and sandals to change into at the end of the day to relieve my blistered feet—and set off on what is still to this day the greatest adventure of my life.

---

20 The word dojo literally means "place of the way" and usually refers to a martial arts training hall.

Before boarding the ferry across to Shikoku, I took the two-hour motorbike ride out to Koyasan, resting place of Kobo Daishi, the great esoteric Shingon Buddhist monk who was born on Shikoku Island in 774 CE. After several years studying and attaining enlightenment in China, he returned to live and die on his island of birth, where he set up or at least visited each of the eighty-eight temples that now form the pilgrimage route. The visit to his resting place before and after the trip is said to give *henro* the protection and merit they need for the arduous journey through some of the most challenging yet glorious terrain in all of Japan.

When I arrived at Temple Number One, Ryozenji, I bought my *kongotsue* (pilgrim's staff) and trail map, which was totally in Japanese. Japan has three alphabets, only two of which I could read, making map reading somewhat challenging at times. I bypassed the other traditional pilgrim's uniform, which consisted of *hakui*—a white, waist-length cotton shirt, which represents a *henro*'s burial shroud, and the conspicuous *sugegasa*—a conical-shaped hat made of straw, representing the *henro*'s coffin, mainly because I just couldn't afford them, but also because I wasn't planning on dying along the way.

Over the next forty days, I experienced the highs and lows, joys and struggles, epiphanies and challenges of walking the *henro* trail. There is nothing like being on the trail on your own, everything you need on your back, totally free to go where you like, no distractions, no responsibilities except to use your core strength and wits to keep yourself alive, fed, clean, and healthy. Days turned into weeks of pushing forward with a clear goal and purpose to achieve, surrounded at all times by the majestic natural masterpiece that is Shikoku Island. You soon get into the trail mind-set: the morning routine, the map reading, the temple routine, the quiet awareness of your mind and surroundings, the search for the small red pilgrim figures painted on lampposts and fences guiding the way, and the "getting ready for sleep" routine.

Once the blisters and the blisters on top of those blisters hardened, my legs just began to carry me, propelled by no more than willpower and an almost robotic commitment to just keep moving forward. I slept in parks and forests, bus stops and train stations, on beaches and benches, in *tsuyado*,[21] in the temples themselves, which often had rooms for pilgrims, and on four or five occasions, I was invited to spend the night with a kind resident who couldn't bear the thought of a pilgrim, especially a *gaijin*[22] one, sleeping on the ground in the local park.

For cleanliness, I bathed in rivers, used showers by the beach, and went into handicap-accessible bathrooms (as they had more space), where I filled up bottles of water from the tap and poured them over my head, and a few times I found hosepipes in public parks to wash off the grime of a full day's walk. I did laundry in sinks and rivers and hung it up to dry between trees or lampposts while I rested, or just draped it over my bag as I walked.

I picked up food along the way in local markets and stores and was often fed and given money as *o-settai* (a donation) by people wanting to gain merit for helping me on my way. I was even invited to join a company for their annual dinner when they ran into me at the train station I was about to make my home for the night. After a lavish five-course meal, I was invited back to sleep at the house of one of the workers, a huge step up from the packet of sushi and train-station bench that was going to be my food and accommodation for the night. I was usually alone on the trail, but for some stretches I found a walking partner—Ken from Tokyo, Yoshi from Kyoto, another from Nara—all who were using their holiday time to notch up their pilgrim miles for that year.

The trail passed through villages, towns, and cities, along beaches, through fields and forests, and, as the most beautiful and peaceful place to build a temple is on top of a mountain, I spent much of my time climbing the winding paths or rock stairs that led up to the sanctuary on top. Forty days after setting out, I arrived back at Ryozenji, Temple Number One. I sat for a while, contemplating and integrating what I had just been through. An epic adventure into Japanese culture, nature, spirituality, and history, and, more significantly, into my Self, my limits, and my mind. On the trail there were so many particulars to think about—food, shelter, map reading, medical supplies—one wrong turn,

---

21 Huts scattered around the island set up especially for *henro* to rest in.

22 Foreigner.

one bad decision, could add hours to the journey; one right one could greatly ease the burdens and reveal the magic the trail had to offer. Once again, walking The Way demonstrated to me the great lesson that little details really can make a big difference...

CHAPTER 10

Israel

Coming Home and Walking the Land

April 17, 2008: I was sitting on a hill just outside of Latrun, a thirty-eight kilometer walk from Jerusalem, two nights before Pesach. We'd just set up camp, the pot was on the fire, someone had whipped out the guitar, someone else was finishing up Minchah.

It was the sixteenth day of our epic All for the Kids fund-raising hike along the Israel National Trail, which runs 1,015 kilometers from Tel Dan on the Lebanese border to Eilat, nine kilometers from the southernmost tip of Israel.

I planned to complete the walk in forty days, based on the story in the Torah[1] in which the spies walked the Land of Israel for forty days and gave a bad report. I wanted to connect to the Land, raise money for orphanages, and do a tikkun (fixing) for the spies by walking the whole country for forty days and giving a good report at the end of it. The guy in the trail office said that forty days was perhaps a bit too fast a pace and that most people did it in around two months. By that time though, there had already been quite a bit of coverage in the Jewish press in

1 *Parashat Shelach, Bamidbar* 13.

several countries in which I mentioned the whole forty-day thing, and it wouldn't have looked so good if it took more than that, so the challenge was laid down.

As we tucked into our dinner of spaghetti with tuna and tomato sauce, it occurred to me that my ancestors living in the Land three thousand years ago most probably spent the night in this very spot, cooking their dinner, a couple of days before completing their pilgrimage into Jerusalem for Pesach. I felt that I was living the next step in the Jewish story, finally connecting to the Land of my ancestors, the paths they walked, the traditions they kept, and the prayers they uttered, in the best way I knew how, by walking the way of the ancient Jewish masters. It was the next major hike on my warrior's journey, following on from the ones on Shikoku Island and in the Himalayas, just that this time 'The Way' felt much more like home.

I'd been living in Asia for six years and felt that it was time for a major change of scenery. My sights rested firmly on Central and South America, in particular some shamanic training in the jungles of Mexico and a canoe adventure down the Amazon, the world's longest river. I decided to make a stopover in Israel for a few weeks to visit some friends and family I hadn't seen for a while. I'd been to Israel several times before—for a couple of weddings, as a representative of the Great Britain Junior table tennis team in the Maccabi Games, and on a one-month Israel tour with a youth movement when I was sixteen. The last time I'd visited was more than twelve years earlier, when I lived in Israel for three months, working on a kibbutz near Netanya and volunteering with kids in Dimona. Having spent much of my time in India hanging out with Israelis, I had plenty of people to visit and couches to crash on during my three-week stay. As I boarded the plane in Tokyo on my way to Israel, little did I know that I'd only actually make it to South America nine years later, as a rabbi leading a group of American Jews on a social-justice and personal-growth trip to Peru. My path was about to take a major turn toward finding the treasure that was buried in my backyard all along.

After spending my first week in Israel being spoiled by my first cousin and his family on their moshav, I decided it was time to head out and see the Land. I remembered that my favorite place was Tsfat—the cool air, maze of streets, expansive views, and lofty spiritual vibe made it feel to me like the Nepal of Israel.

On the way up, I stopped off to stay in a kibbutz next to the Kinneret with an Israeli friend I had met on my travels. I spent my time hanging out with the guys there, most of whom had just come back from their post-army trip around the world. We sat around all day playing guitars and bongos, chatting, eating, and going to a local spring to cool off in the midday heat—throw in some rice and *dahl* and you could have convinced me I'd landed back in India. There was one religious guy there, David, who was very interested in my travels, and on hearing that I'd spent many years studying other religions asked me why I hadn't learned about Judaism. I replied honestly that although I had a strong Jewish identity, Judaism seemed to me a pretty irrelevant, outdated, elitist, ritualistic, dogmatic, male chauvinistic, closed-minded, fear- and guilt-based, unspiritual religion, and that religious people didn't seem to me to be too connected or even particularly friendly. It was a decent list.

In fact, it is because of these factors that most Jews who are seeking a more spiritual path in life go to Eastern religions, which seem much more compassionate, open, loving, and spiritual. I read one figure that forty percent of practicing Buddhists in America are actually Jewish. It doesn't surprise me; Judaism definitely needs a new PR team. David said he could really see why I would think all those things, but that maybe I just perceived Judaism like that because I had never really learned in more depth what it actually believes and teaches.

After two weeks there, it was time to make the journey up to Tsfat. David told me about a cheap youth hostel called Ascent where I could hang out, go on hikes, meet other young people, and take classes in

Jewish mysticism. By the time I arrived it was after dark, and as soon as I stepped off the bus, I felt the calm and spiritual uplift that I still feel whenever I visit this holy city. I walked toward Ascent, and as I turned on to the road, I could hear some loud music in the near distance—but nothing prepared me for what I was about to walk into. Rather than a quiet, mystical hostel, I arrived at a crazy Chassidic party, vodka flowing freely, a live band, and hundreds of Jews of all types singing and dancing in circles. I was welcomed with open arms and a glass of vodka and discovered that they were celebrating *Yud Tet Kislev*, the "New Year" for Chabad Chassidim and also the yahrzeit of the Baal Shem Tov's main disciple and successor, Dov Ber, the Maggid of Mezritch.

After the warm welcome and another *l'chaim* or two, one of the Chassidim asked me what my Hebrew name is. "Ber," I replied. I was named after my grandfather, Bernard, who had passed away long before I was born. They looked a bit confused. "Ber isn't a real Hebrew name. Your name must be Dov Ber," they exclaimed excitedly.

Okay, I thought, *whatever*. It seemed to make them happy and everyone had another *l'chaim*.

I ended up spending a month living at Ascent in exchange for doing some writing work and helping other guests settle in. During the day, I volunteered at Livnot U'Lehibanot, an incredible organization specializing in a mix of hiking, volunteering, and Jewish learning, where I spent my time helping to rebuild a school that had been damaged by a bomb in the Lebanon War earlier that year. In my spare time, I took classes on Judaism, both at Ascent and at a Chabad yeshiva up the hill, and I connected to some young American students studying at Yeshivat Shalom Rav, where I was allowed to sit in on some of their classes.

These were the first real religious Jews I had come into contact with, and I was pretty impressed by their integrity, warmth, intelligence, and general attitude to life. I was welcomed into homes for Shabbat meals, people were always open to answering questions, and I was introduced to a whole world of Jewish wisdom and practice that I had been unaware of—including putting on tefillin for the first time in my life (at the age of twenty-nine).

After a while, someone suggested I meet Yonah Akiva, an American chassid who learned all day in the large Breslov shul overlooking the ancient cemetery. I made my way down through the web of alleyways and entered the study hall, which was full of people wearing black coats, with long curly *peyot* and beards, shouting at each other about whatever was written in the large tomes filled with Hebrew and Aramaic writing open in front of them. I found Yonah, who greeted me warmly and offered me a seat opposite him. He shared a bit about his life growing up in a secular home in Boston, going to college in Massachusetts, and volunteering in the inner-city Peace Corps before coming to Israel, where he lived on a kibbutz for a few months. He took a few classes in Jewish philosophy but then left to travel through Egypt, Jordan, India, and Nepal for half a year, after which he decided to head back to Israel. A few more classes turned into a few years of learning, during which time he moved up to Tsfat, found a community he connected to, got married, had several kids, and now spends the majority of his day teaching and learning Torah. It was amazing to me that someone who had lived a "normal" life and even traveled a bit had eventually chosen to go down this path. It was nearly Chanukah, so we decided to learn something about the upcoming holiday. Of course, I knew the Chanukah story—the Maccabees, the oil in the Temple, and that we light candles and eat doughnuts, but that was about it.

Yonah opened the book in front of him[2] and started to read and translate. I don't think I've ever seen anyone so passionate and alive with what he was learning and teaching. Suddenly, Chanukah wasn't just a nice festival commemorating what happened a long time ago; it had powerful contemporary meaning and significance. I don't even really remember what he said, but it was something about Chanukah being the pinnacle of the year, with this supernal energy coming down and the flames of the candles effecting the higher worlds and connecting us to our souls, which are a piece of the Divine soul, and so on and so on. I couldn't believe what I was hearing. A religious Jew talking about G-d-consciousness, mindfulness, and personal development! It was a far cry from the image I had created of religious Jews walking around somewhat miserably, doing a bunch of outdated rituals out of fear of punishment.

---

2 *Likutei Halachot*.

Chanukah finished, and I went back to learn again—I believe it was a Wednesday. I sat down opposite Yonah and he said, "I'm glad you came today, because in many ways Wednesday is the pinnacle of the week! This energy is coming down, Shabbat is beginning..." and once again I was whisked off into a world of wonder, passion, profound insight, and joyful connection to the Divine energies and purpose of life. I walked out of there into the serene mystical energy, crisp air, and clear skies of Tsfat, winding my way through quaint cobbled lanes, past vibrant study halls and synagogues, small children with *kippot* and *peyot* running home from school, surrounded by beautiful views of the Kinneret and Mount Meron.

I found a quiet spot on the top of a hill to meditate, gently closed my eyes, and although I was far from convinced of anything, I felt a deep yearning to find out more about what my own tradition teaches about the nature of reality. As I settled into my practice, I felt my heart opening and my soul awakening and I started to get the feeling that maybe, just maybe, I'd stumbled upon exactly the thing I had been looking for since beginning my warrior's journey in my small apartment in Manchester University seven years earlier.

After just over a month, someone suggested that I go to Aish HaTorah in Jerusalem, a yeshiva especially set up to share the basics of traditional Judaism with those who didn't grow up in observant homes. There I could learn the foundations of Jewish philosophy and practice, ask whatever questions I had, and interact with Jews from all backgrounds, while getting to live in the heart of the Old City of Jerusalem. It sounded like a reasonable plan, so I packed up, made my way down south from the city of air to the city of fire,[3] checked into The Heritage House,[4] and made my way to the Kotel for the first time in twelve years. Although I didn't have a spontaneous spiritual experience like many other people do, I definitely felt the sanctity of the area and enjoyed meditating in

3 There are four holy cities in Israel and they are related to the four elements. Jerusalem is the city of fire, Tsfat is the city of air, Chevron is earth, and Tiveria is water.

4 A free hostel for Jewish travelers in the Old City of Jerusalem.

the sunlight, opposite the wall that had seen hundreds of thousands of prayers, tears, songs, and dances throughout the generations. Someone pointed me toward Aish, and I popped in for a few classes, which continued to reshape the stereotype I had created of Judaism and religious Jews. After a couple of days, I was offered a place in the dorms—and that was when the red lights started to go off back home!

Sadly, very often when a child starts to become more religious it can cause tremendous issues for the family. It can be pretty scary for parents who imagine that their kid is getting brainwashed and joining a cult, or hurtful that they seem to be going against the values they were brought up with. Parents worry that their kid is going to end up dressing strangely, becoming unrelatable, and refusing to eat in their home, and all in all, it can feel like they are losing their child.

In almost all cases, this is not what happens. Over the years, I have seen that almost invariably, after the initial worries and struggles, in any family that had a strong bond to begin with—where the kids are sensible and sensitive and the parents are open and supportive—it all works itself out in the end. Once the parents see that the kids have remained basically who they were before and have not become cult members and that they are actually spending time working on their character traits, becoming kinder and happier and trying to the live the healthiest, most meaningful life they can, things smooth out and settle down (especially once the grandkids start arriving!). Of course, an unhealthy person who "finds religion" just becomes an unhealthy religious person. I was always taught that the more one becomes spiritually refined, connected, and works on improving himself and his character traits, the less judgmental and the more open, accepting, and loving he becomes. Therefore, when a person starts becoming more religious and begins putting down other types of Jews, especially their family, it means they haven't actually become more religious, they've just become self-righteous.

When a person starts becoming more religious and begins putting down other types of Jews, especially their family, it means they haven't actually become more religious, they've just become self-righteous.

I turned up in yeshiva, kind of hoping to show the rabbis how naive and backward they were by sharing with them the insights I had learned on my journey through the East. I debated with rabbis from all backgrounds and walks of life, some of whom had become religious at a later age, others who grew up in religious families, all of whom seemed to be highly intelligent and well-thought-out. After a while, I noticed that all the ideas I was sharing with them they'd either refute with very sound logic or go and get a book from the shelf and say, "Totally! The Vilna Gaon says that here in *Even Sheleimah*..." or, "The Ramchal speaks about it in *Derech Hashem*..."

I started to realize that the reason I had not been attracted to Judaism was that I had a very superficial understanding of what Judaism actually believes.

The truth is, I was pretty taken aback and humbled. These were guys with great character traits, profound wisdom, worldly knowledge, and who seemed to be living conscious and joyful lives. Far from brainwashing, I found it to be a very open environment, no pressure, no judgements, just a bunch of guys delving into themselves and their heritage, grappling with the purpose of life.

I started to realize that the reason I had not been attracted to Judaism was that I had a very superficial understanding of what Judaism actually believes.

Some people seem to equate religion with irrationality, blind faith, and neediness, as opposed to the rational, modern, scientific worldview of the twenty-first century. And yet, here I found very rational and intelligent people tackling the questions of life from a philosophical, scientific, and highly spiritual point of view, which was in no way a contradiction. I carried on learning and questioning and debating, and three weeks turned into three months. I formed great friendships with the other guys as I got a taste of yeshiva life for the first time, friendships I still have to this day. Instead of teasing each other and putting each other down, which seemed to me the main mode of communication among guys back home, we built up a strong comradery, supporting each other on our journey, learning, singing, drinking, and, of course, playing football together.

Living in the Old City was intense and magical. We went on trips to see other parts of the Land, and I went to my first Orthodox wedding, which was so moving, with such palpable holiness, that my eyes filled up with tears for the first time in many years. I experienced the festivals and Shabbat in a deeper way, having learned more about them, and started to find the joy in Jewish ritual and practice.

My parents came to visit to see what I was getting myself into and were as amazed as I was that our impression of yeshiva being a dark, morose place of old men with long beards hunched over books, no sunlight, bare rations, and rats running around couldn't have been further from the truth. They joined us for some classes and my father shared with us all how impressed he was with the guys, the teachers, and the atmosphere. Although it may not have been the path my parents had hoped for me, their fears were alleviated, and they were completely supportive, as they had been throughout my life.[5]

I starting going to some of the prayer services, and having learned about some special rabbis with the name Dov Ber, I decided to be called to the Torah with that name. For me, having a Hebrew name helped me reidentify myself with who I ideally wanted to be rather than stay stuck in the persona I had created for myself growing up. It was a very special time, surrounded by good people, all questioning life, consciously working on ourselves, having uplifting classes and discussions, and getting to experience living within the walls of the ancient city where many of the stories we were learning about took place.

And then it was enough.

It all just seemed a bit too good to be true. Although I was far from being a naive, vulnerable teenager who could be swept away in it all, I felt the need to get out of there for a breather, to gain a new perspective on where my journey was taking me and reconnect with what I thought and felt to be right when not surrounded by it all.

---

5 At one point I was talking to my mum about how great the learning and life was, and she said, "But you're not wearing a *kippah*, are you?" A few months later I was expressing that I was struggling with some of the ideas, and she said, "But you're still wearing your *kippah*, aren't you?" She could clearly see a positive change in me.

My sister was living in Malawi, a small country next to Mozambique in Southern Africa, where she was working as a doctor and researcher in one of the main hospitals. She'd been asking me for a long time to visit, and this seemed to be the perfect opportunity; I hadn't seen her for quite a while and had never experienced Africa (outside of South Africa). So I packed my bags, bid farewell to my friends and rabbis, and headed out to realign myself and take stock of my life in the Warm Heart of Africa.

Notwithstanding our very different life choices, my sister Danielle and I have been extremely close since our late teens. We'd already traveled together in Sri Lanka, Thailand, Japan, Korea, Bali, and India, so I relished spending time hanging out with her, getting a glimpse into her life, and experiencing a whole new country and culture.

She arranged for me to volunteer at the Kuunika Foundation, a school for impoverished children on the outskirts of Blantyre, and each morning I'd get the local bus out to the village, comfortably back in my familiar role as the only white man, just this time I was called *mzungu* instead of *farang* or *gaijin*.

I spent my days teaching English and helping with the farming, as well as writing a business plan and doing some fund-raising for them. On weekends, my sister and I would travel around the country, visiting Lake Malawi, Mulanje Mountain, one of the many exquisite tea plantations, or just hanging out around town, going to live music events and drinking in the local backpacker hangout.

I spent some time every day reading the Jewish books I'd brought along with me, including *Derech Hashem* by the Ramchal and *Living Inspired* by Rabbi Akiva Tatz. I made Kiddush every Friday night (on non-kosher wine), avoided all seafood, and didn't have ice cream after eating (non-kosher) chicken or beef. It was a very important time for me to return to balance, realign with my values, and integrate where I had come from into where I seemed to be moving. There were many things pulling me in all directions. I wasn't ready to commit to all the things Judaism would demand of me, and I still had dreams of visiting South

America and canoeing down the Yukon in Alaska. Yet after a wonderful couple of months, it started becoming clear that I had some unfinished business in Israel. My soul was being called back to the Holy Land, and so once again I packed my bags, boarded the plane to Tel Aviv,[6] and the rest, as they say, is "His" story.

One evening, as my mum and auntie were preparing supper in my auntie's house, I asked them what their father's Hebrew name was. His English name was Bernard, and I was named after him. My auntie, who at that point didn't know my Hebrew name, told me—and I was not at all surprised to hear—that his name was (of course!) Dov Ber.

It was after about four months of learning for around fifteen hours a day in yeshiva, gradually taking on more things in a slow and healthy process, that I felt it was time for another major adventure, and my sights turned toward the Israel National Trail. Almost 150 kilometers shorter than the Shikoku Trail, it seemed very doable. Also, it was an excellent opportunity to really get to know the Land, which by that time I was already pretty sure would become my home. This time, instead of just walking, I was inspired to raise money for the orphanages I had worked with around the world, as well as some organizations in Israel.

Every night I would huddle over my computer in the dorm room at Aish and brainstorm the project. Websites, fund-raising, logistics, routes, press releases—once my mind locks on a plan, I become obsessed and make sure it happens. Everything started falling into place, and the project took on a life of its own. The start date was set, the articles starting appearing in the Jewish press around the world, and it was all systems go. My roommate, Jeremy, and another guy at Aish, Yonatan, decided to come on board pretty last minute, and so with the strong driving spirit of adventure, some great company, and clear goals, we set off to traverse the entire Land of our forefathers.

6 Via Johannesburg.

I could really write a whole book about the walk. It's totally remarkable that in one small country spanning just 424 kilometers from north to south,[7] there are snowcapped mountains, forests, beaches, cities, and deserts. I'd tell about some of the grueling treks up Mount Hermon, Mount Tabor, and Mount Carmel, about the "Trail Angels"—people who offered food and accommodation to trail hikers—the time we bumped into a group of Thai farmers celebrating Songkran (their New Year) and their shock as I joined in singing their traditional songs with them. We had a joint walk along the Netanya promenade with the Forgotten People's Fund, and visited Sderot to do activities and give out teddy bears to school kids affected by the constant bombings.

I'd love to describe all the locals and the other hikers we met on the way, the places we slept, the weather conditions we faced, the food we ate—including, on several occasions, very fresh, still very warm milk straight from goats' udders into our bottles, donated by friendly Bedouin farmers. Of course, I'd write about the time I woke up in the desert in the middle of the night to see my stuff strewn all around and looked up to behold the Arabian wolf, who had caused the mess, silhouetted against the night sky, staring me out from about eighty meters away, and how I ran out of water, ten kilometers from Eilat, on my own, in scorching heat.

By the time we arrived in Eilat, we'd raised eighteen thousand dollars for two charities in Israel, Beit HaYeled and The Forgotten People's Fund, and Kuunika in Malawi. It was a pretty hot day, and once I met the others who had taken a different route, we walked straight to the beach and dived into the warm waters of the Red Sea, a welcome relief after walking over a thousand kilometers to get there. We found a campground to sleep in that night and spent Shabbat with the Chief Rabbi of Eilat and his family.

On Sunday, we parted ways and I caught the bus back to Jerusalem. As we sped along the road, rushing effortlessly past the same kilometers, where at some points each unshaded step along rocky wadis or up

---

7 The trail itself is over one thousand kilometers, as it zigzags across the country.

jagged cliffs had become a challenge, I had mixed emotions. Triumph, accomplishment, and contentment on the one hand, yet on the other, sadness at being off the trail and emptiness as the whole project that I had invested so much time and heart into had come to an end. But by the time I arrived back in Jerusalem, covering in just four hours by bus what had taken me three weeks to walk in the other direction, I was already planning my next All for the Kids social-justice adventure, one which would take me back to the vast subcontinent of India.

CHAPTER 11

Why Judaism?

The challenge of this world is not finding the truth, that's pretty obvious.[1] The challenge is having the courage to live with integrity after you know it.

Rabbi Leib Kelemen

The most common question that I get asked is why, after everything I saw, experienced, and learned, I ended up devoting my life to Torah Judaism. Personally, I used to think that people who become religious do so either because they are young and impressionable, susceptible to brainwashing, or lacking in happiness and meaning and therefore looking for a crutch. Yet when I landed in Israel, I had no intention of even studying Judaism. I was a well-educated and experienced twenty-nine-year-old, not particularly susceptible to brainwashing, and I was living a very happy and meaningful life.

So what did I see and learn that made me make such a drastic turnaround?

As I have shared throughout the pages of this book, I have found Torah Judaism to be the perfect system for us to derive the most meaning and depth out of every area of our lives, to achieve our purpose, reach our potential, correct our character flaws, find authentic joy, and make sure we are conscientiously reaching out to improve the world

1 Once you've taken a serious look at the evidence.

around us. Through Jewish Law—which deals with every area of life, from the moment we wake up to the moment we go to sleep—there is nothing, no matter how mundane, that can't be done in a conscious and intentional way, which imbues everything we do throughout the day with depth and meaning.

LIFE-CYCLE EVENTS

I have seen that all major life events, transitions, and relationships are set up so that we can get the most out of them. For example, *aveilut*, the laws of mourning, help us deal with our loss in an empowered and emotionally intelligent way. When someone passes away, it's easy to either fall into depression, or the opposite—to deny it and just say, "It's all for the best," "They've gone on to a better place," or "They'd want me to be happy." Judaism says that neither of these attitudes is healthy and healing. It may well be "all for the best" in the big picture, but that doesn't stop the pain. An integral part of the healing is to first take time to fully feel the pain, sadness, anger, or guilt of the loss, hence the prescribed time period of seven days in which we sit on low chairs, people come and speak about the departed, and we come very intensely face-to-face with our grief. Then comes a thirty-day period of less intense mourning, and then eleven months of saying Kaddish, plus doing mitzvot and other positive acts in honor of the departed—all of which helps us gradually process our loss and move on, hopefully to turn our pain and loss into purpose and growth.

The laws of family purity, which restrict the physical relationship between a husband and wife during certain times, exist not because intimacy is frowned upon, but quite the opposite. It's because of the great sanctity of marriage that the laws are specifically designed to create a relationship that is full and loving and as spiritually, physically, intellectually, and emotionally intimate as possible. In fact, many people in the secular world are starting to put this into practice as a way to keep their relationships strong, respectful, and truly intimate. Added to this is that partners in a marriage do not express affection for anyone else of the opposite gender. A friend once said to me that it's a bit extreme that I don't touch other women, to which I replied that it may be extreme, but that's exactly what's creating an extremely beautiful and holy relationship with my wife.

PERSONAL GROWTH

I've also learned that Judaism provides the ultimate year-round personal-growth seminar. So much Torah law focuses on working on becoming *tzaddikim*: not bearing a grudge, not speaking *lashon hara*, loving your fellow as yourself, and the whole *mussar* movement, which is devoted to personal growth and perfection of character traits. I started to see that the festivals themselves are intensified pockets of time to work on particular aspects of our lives.

We celebrate Pesach not just to commemorate our ancestors leaving slavery in Egypt thousands of years ago, but rather to tap into the energy of being able to leave behind our own slavery and limitations now. The Hebrew word for Egypt is Mitzrayim, which comes from the root word *meitzarim*, meaning boundaries or limitations. All the laws and customs exist to help us tap into this; for example, we eat matzah, which is dry and flat, to signify overcoming the puffed-up ego, represented by bread.

Chanukah is not just about commemorating that our ancestors found some oil in the Temple thousands of years ago; it is for us to tap into the understanding that just as a candle lit in the dark can bring so much light and warmth into us (Chanukah is at the darkest time of year), so too our greatest breakthroughs and light come from overcoming our darkest challenges (represented by the Greeks).

In this way each festival comes to help us consciously work on a particular part of ourselves.

PRACTICAL AND GROUNDED

I also appreciate that Judaism is more practical, grounded, and in line with our experience of reality than many other religions. Rather than teaching detachment from the world, Judaism encourages us to take part in it fully—to get married, have a job, enjoy good food, music, exercise, and nature. Torah law is not only about Shabbat and *kashrut* and lofty spiritual things that take a much higher level of consciousness to even begin to understand, but rather things such as tzedakah and business ethics, all aimed at creating a healthy society where the vulnerable are taken care of. Rather than distancing ourselves from the world, we are here to uplift and perfect it.

LIFESTYLE AND VALUES

The lifestyle and values that I saw people living by also really attracted me. I went to my rabbis' houses for Shabbat meals and saw a whole world in which there was less focus on material gratification, I met kids who didn't spend hours in front of the TV, who were reading children's books teaching about developing good character traits, with heroes who were *tzaddikim* rather than men who are really great at kicking a football but who don't necessarily live the most morally upright lives off the field.

Certainly, the Orthodox world is not perfect, and like all communities, it has its issues. Yet I've noticed that these are problems that stem from human nature and they exist in all communities all over the world; they have nothing to do with the Torah and its teachings.

SELF-REALIZATION

I also used to think that to be observant, I had to give up my self-expression in order to fit into a rigid system, yet I saw that within the structured guidelines of Jewish law there is plenty of room for self-expression. Just like everyone on the football pitch is playing to the same rules, yet each player has their particular style, expression, skill set, and role, so too, I saw observant Jews with long *peyot*, short *peyot*, no *peyot*, black *kippot*, knitted *kippot*, white tzitzit, blue tzitzit, black hat, no hat, baseball cap, farming all day, learning all day, learning and working, going to the army, not going to the army...I soon realized that there is no set way to be an observant Jew and I appreciated that I did not need to leave behind who I was and what I'd experienced; I could integrate it into a higher expression of my true self.

However, the most fundamental piece of the puzzle was that I finally got a solid answer to the question I had posed to each group of people I had met along the way. I loved, and still do really appreciate, all the philosophies and practices I came into contact with throughout my journey. They each have insightful teachings and uplifting practices. I find that some people are hoping I'll belittle other religions, but I'd rather inspire people to connect to Judaism by sharing its depth, beauty, and authenticity than by putting down other paths. (Someone who is confident and at peace with their path doesn't need to raise themselves up by putting others down.) Yet there was one question that always came up for me when studying religions and philosophies: how do you know you're right?

Of course, being right doesn't make you nicer, more spiritual, or a better person than anyone else. In fact, thinking you are right often makes people self-righteous, arrogant, and can even lead to war. At the same time, I knew they couldn't all be right and I wanted to find out which one I should devote my life to.

Gandhi, when asked if he was a Hindu, replied, "Yes, I am. I'm also a Buddhist, a Christian, a Muslim, and a Jew." Now, I'm sure he didn't mean that literally and was just trying to make an important point about universalism, yet really it just doesn't make any sense. Each path believes very different things. The Buddhists taught the doctrine of *anatta*—non-self, the Vedantans taught *atta*—you do have a soul. The Christians said Jesus, the Muslims said Mohammed. They couldn't all be right. In all my time exploring the traditions of the world, no one could give me a solid answer to my question: How do you know you're right? How do you know this is actually true? Just because it feels right, sounds right, someone told you it's right, I hope/want/need it to be right is not good enough. Answers such as "My master told me," "I came to the insight through meditation," "It seems logical," or "You just have to believe," just didn't do it for me, as there was no rational basis for the belief. He found non-self in his meditation and he found Jesus in his, his master told him one thing, his told him another. Solid intellectual belief has to be based on empirical, logical, scientific, verifiable evidence. Until this point, I hadn't found any to support any of the paths I was looking into.

Until I arrived in Israel.

For the first time, when I posed my question, "How do you know you're right?" I came into contact with empirical, rational, scientific, and historical evidence that the holy books of the Jewish People could not have been written without some pretty serious intervention from an existence beyond time and space, one that can make miraculous claims, knows every creature in the whole of existence, and is in control of history. Although there are great spiritual truths and mystical ideas written in the holy books of all religions, there are none that a highly conscious human couldn't have come up with.

And the truly amazing thing was that the evidence was so sound, it actually overcame my confirmation bias.[2] I didn't want it to be true! I still wanted to travel, try out many different things, and there were certain things in Judaism that didn't resonate with me at the time. However, after six months of grappling with it, enlisting the help of atheist forums and anyone else who would listen, I just couldn't refute the evidence.[3]

Of course, like with everything else in life, there is no 100-percent proof, but there is enough evidence to take it far beyond any reasonable doubt. After several months of debating and arguing and resisting, I finally admitted that the intellectually honest thing to do would be to commit to the system that had proven itself not just to be deep, beautiful, and empowering if followed in a conscious and joyful way, but also the only one that had real evidence pointing toward its veracity. Someone once said to me that I'm crazy for believing this stuff. I thought about it and replied, "Some things I believe in may seem a bit crazy, but I'm certainly not crazy for believing them—the evidence is all there."

So, about nine months after I first started learning in Israel, around Rosh Hashanah time, I decided it was time to start taking things to the next level. I still had questions and doubts, but whenever they arose I would just go through the evidence again in my mind, reaffirming the strong foundations of my belief. Yet it was still only another eight

---

2 People find evidence for what they want to believe and ignore the evidence that goes against their beliefs.

3 For two out of at least five highly compelling pieces of evidence that the Torah cannot have been written by a human being, check out www.areyouright.org.

months later, on Shavuot, that I finally committed fully to receiving the gift of the Torah and devoting my life to living with its advice. The Enlightened Jewish Master-in-training had finally met his true Master.

And that's where the real work began.

CHAPTER 12

Soulmates

Verse One:

A new baal teshuvah, I'd finally found the truth of reality,
But there was one thing missing, the other half of me,
Shteiging in the Beis, davening every day
That Hashem would bring her my way,
And then one day there she came,
Walking through the rain
And I knew that my life would never be the same...

Chorus:

Oriana Devorah,
You make me wanna learn Torah,
Chassidus, halachah, and Gemara,
You know I'd do anything for ya.

Verse Two

I wanna build a bayis ne'eman,
And have lots of daughters and lots of sons,
And I wanna house that is filled with shalom,
And work together toward Tikkun Olam,
And I'm just so glad that our wedding day has come,
And our neshamos have finally become one.
So we'll sing and we'll dance and we'll have so much fun,
As we give our thanks to the Ribono Shel Olam.

Chorus:
Oriana Devorah,
You make me wanna learn Torah,
Chassidus, halachah, and Gemara,
You know I'd do anything for ya,
And I hope I never bore ya,
And I promise I'll never ignore ya—bli neder,
Always be there to reassure ya,
And you know I totally adore ya,
Together we'll light the menorah,
And you got the most beautiful aura...Oriana Devorah.

"Oriana Devorah," as performed at our wedding, 7 Tammuz, 5769 (2009)

Just over two years after I arrived in Israel, on December 13, 2008, I met the woman who, according to Jewish tradition, was ordained for me forty days before I began to take form in the womb.[1] I'd been learning full-time[2] in yeshiva for a couple of years and felt ready to take the next step. Since becoming observant, I had been set up with seven different girls, each of them wonderful in their own way, but none that I felt the need to go on another date with. Then one Friday night, I was having Shabbat dinner at a friend's house, where we each shared a little about ourselves by way of introduction. One of the other guests, Nati, approached me during the meal and said that he knew the perfect girl for me. She had just recently become observant after being into Eastern religions. She was a yoga teacher, healer, social worker, and artist and was born in South Africa like my parents. It sounded pretty promising until he told me that she had been learning in Jerusalem for a year and had just left back to South Africa literally the night before. He assured me it was a great match and he'd connect us via email. I told him that as nice as it sounded, I

1 *Sotah* 2a.
2 With a couple of breaks to go to Malawi and walk the Israel National Trail.

didn't want an email address or a long-distance relationship. I wanted a wife. And we left it at that.

I was sitting at home with a close friend on *motzaei Shabbat* when my phone rang. I picked up and was surprised to hear Nati's excited voice. "I thought you guys were so good for each other, so I called her in case I had gotten the date wrong, and she picked up the phone!"

He went on to tell me that in fact he hadn't got the date wrong at all, she *was* meant to leave on Thursday night. It turned out that she had gone to the airport and got to the front of the queue, where she was duly informed that the flight had been rescheduled. Upon inquiring when the flight would be, she was informed that it had left the night before! I'd heard of flights being postponed for a few days, but I'd never heard of one being put forward by a day. She was also a little confused as to why she wasn't informed about this, but made her way back to Jerusalem, thinking that obviously Hashem had some reason He wanted her to spend one more Shabbat in Israel. That thought was validated when she got a call telling her about a great guy she had to meet. It was now or never, as they had put her on the Sunday night flight.

So I headed out to meet "the perfect girl for me." We met at the King David Hotel and walked through a slight drizzle to a quaint café overlooking the walls of the Old City. The main difference between this girl and the seven girls I had been set up on dates with before her was that with the others it had taken me under five minutes to see that they weren't my wife, but with this one I was pretty sure within about four minutes that she actually most likely was. We chatted for a few hours, and by the time I dropped her back at her seminary, I knew my search was over.

We met the next morning and decided that, although it was a bit intense, she should postpone her flight so we'd have a few more days to date before I left to England on Thursday to spend time with my parents. She arrived at the El Al office, and when her turn came, she told them she wanted to push off her flight that night. After inquiring after her name and searching on the computer, the guy looked up and told her that it appeared she wasn't even on that flight; they must have forgotten to give her a seat. Clearly, Hashem was working His magic again through His favorite airline. We had another wonderful date and another one on Tuesday morning before she flew back home that evening.

I went back to England to spend Chanukah with my parents and told my mom about meeting an amazing girl. I was describing her when my mom suddenly asked expectantly, "What's her name?" When she heard that her name was Oriana, my mother literally jumped off her chair and said, "It's *bashert*!" I was a little confused, as I was pretty sure my mother isn't a kabbalist or a prophetess. She filled me in that three months earlier she'd been in Johannesburg having lunch with her close friend from school. Her friend's daughter-in-law was there, and as my mom started speaking about me and my journey, the daughter-in-law told her that one of her best friends had a very similar story and was studying in Jerusalem as well. It turns out that the *shidduch* had already been thought of and my mom was already in on it! For a few reasons, they hadn't followed through with setting it up, so Hashem was forced to find other ways to make sure we'd meet.

About a week later, while I was still in London and Oriana was in Jo'burg, we were chatting and she asked me how I thought it was going. She was wondering if we should still try to make it work or maybe date other people in the meantime. I thought about it for a bit and replied, quite matter-of-factly, "I think you'll come back to Israel soon and we'll date and get married in June."

This, quite reasonably, freaked her out a little bit.

However, the hand of Divine Providence was on my side once again, as, having put the phone down, she remembered that earlier that year she had been camping with a friend near Mitzpe Ramon and had had a vivid dream that she would get married the next year in—you got it—June. We dated long distance for two months, with a little breakup and makeup in the middle (nothing better than a breakup and makeup to cement a relationship!) and eventually she arrived back in Israel on Rosh Chodesh Adar—a great reason to increase my joy.

A few weeks later, on our way back from an enchanting Shabbat in Tsfat, when everyone else on the bus was asleep, we were chatting quietly, when I said, "You know, it's pretty difficult making it financially in

Israel." She looked at me, smiled, and said, "Don't worry, I think *we'll* be okay." It seemed to really be happening, and, with all the pieces in place, we got engaged a few days later on Rosh Chodesh Nissan, tapping into the power of new beginnings.

You may think it was pretty normal from then on as we made wedding plans and hung out in Jerusalem, but as a forerunner to our lives, eight days later, she was back in South Africa preparing to make Aliyah, and I was in India, running the pilot program of All for the Kids' second project, Be a Kli.[3] I arrived back in Israel two months later, which was just three weeks before the wedding. From the day we met until our wedding was just over six months, four months of which we were in different countries! Our holy and magical wedding was held outdoors in Beit Guvrin on 7 Tammuz, 2009, which in the Gregorian calendar fell out on the twenty-ninth of—you guessed it—June.

In all the ways that it's important to be similar, Oriana Devorah and I are exactly the same. In terms of our values and beliefs, our passion for Torah, Israel, healthy living, and spirituality, we are totally aligned. We are both committed to growth, both personally and as a couple, we are focused on what we can give to rather than what we can get from the relationship, and we use an amazing tool called "grown-up communication" when we are upset with each other, rather than arguing and putting each other down.

Yet personality-wise, you probably couldn't meet two more different people. While she's quiet, graceful, and calm (someone once said to me, "Your wife doesn't walk, she floats!"), I'm generally jumping around, wrestling with kids, and singing and dancing around the house. *Shalom bayit* (peace in the home) doesn't come from people becoming the same, it comes from learning how the different energies can work together to complement and complete each other. Rabbi Aryeh Pamensky gives an incredibly clear and empowering definition of marriage: Marriage is a commitment to putting in the effort to maintain constant emotional

3 See next chapter.

intimacy. That involves checking in to see how connected we are and feel, and if there is any blockage, working out and implementing whatever it takes to regain the closeness.

Here are our top five Enlightened Jewish Master couple keys to a healthy relationship, whether you are looking for someone or are already married:

1. The relationship must be based on sharing similar core values.
2. *Chessed* must be the main character trait: always supporting and looking to give to the other.
3. Grown-up communication: Never speak when you are upset or angry. Find space to process, then come together and share observations, feelings, needs, and requests without blaming the other person.
4. Growth-oriented: Each person must be working on personal and spiritual growth and be committed to investing energy into the relationship.
5. There must be some chemistry/physical attraction.[4]

In our case, it seems that Hashem put the bee[5] and the bear[6] together to enjoy the sweet honey of life.

People often ask me what type of Jews we are, what group we identify with. The truth is that we don't fully fit into or identify with any one of them. We are comfortable in all settings, learning and growing from each of them. One of my *rebbis* is a Belzer Chassid, one is a Litvak who's been learning in the Mir for twenty-five years. I have many *yeshivish* mentors in Aish HaTorah, and a *dati leumi rebbi* in my neighborhood.

4 For more on this, listen to my class at www.soundcloud.com/dov-ber-cohen/relationships.

5 The Hebrew word *devorah* means "bee."

6 The Yiddish word *ber* means "bear."

Whereas in the past this may have seemed wishy-washy and noncommittal, for the new *baal teshuvah* community the opposite is true. It's not that we can't work out which path to choose, it's that regardless of *hashkafah*, once we see someone holding strongly in halachah and authentic *avodat Hashem*, and implementing the approach that works for them, we're willing to learn from all of them and take the best from all worlds. No school is perfect, so we send our kids to the one closest to our *hashkafah* and rely on the main life education taking place, usually by example, at home. When pushed, I've taken to defining myself as CJO: Consciously and Joyously Observant. I'll learn from whatever is going to help me develop myself and come closer to living with Hashem and Torah, building myself and the world around me. Our community in Jerusalem is made up of young committed *baalei teshuvah*, most of whom have made aliyah and are working together to raise their children with a belief in themselves, the Jewish People, Torah, and a deep commitment to living a conscious and joyous way of life, strongly devoted to halachah and *avodat Hashem*.

B'ezrat Hashem, we will all have the merit to raise a new generation of empowered, joyful, inspired, and inspiring Enlightened Jewish Master Kids.

Our daughter Tamara Menucha was born in a hospital, which was a horrible experience for my wife. When she became pregnant again, we decided that this time we'd have a home birth. We worked with the midwife for a few months, making sure everything was healthy and going well. Around three weeks before the due date, the midwife told us that at some time in the coming week or so, she would not be on call as she had a pressing personal matter to deal with. We weren't to worry; it would only be for a short time and we still had plenty of time until the due date, and she gave us the number of another midwife just in case. On Wednesday the next week we welcomed a guest into our home. Rachel, a friend of a friend, was making aliyah and we offered to let her stay in our house for a while until she found her own place. Our friend told us that she was a doula,[7] which would be an extra bonus if we needed her to help with the birth.

On *motzaei Shabbat*, December 28, 2013, Oriana went into labor. We called the midwife and there was no answer. It seemed that things were progressing pretty fast, so I went to get Rachel to check everything. We kept calling the midwife and the replacement one, to no avail. It looked like despite all the preparation we would have to forego the home birth and go to the hospital instead. When we suggested this to Rachel, she wondered why we'd do that when we could just have it at home. When I told her that, with all due respect, we needed a midwife not a doula, she looked confused. "I'm not a doula, I'm a fully qualified home birth midwife. I've delivered 250 babies and have all my equipment downstairs."

So three days after moving into our house, we watched the amazing hand of Divine Providence work its magic once again, as Rachel came upstairs and helped deliver Binyamin Yeshayahu into our lives.

---

7 A doula, also known as a birth coach, is a nonmedical person who stays with and assists a woman before, during, or after childbirth to provide emotional support and physical help if needed (Wikipedia).

CHAPTER 13

Back to the East

Diary entry from the beginning of my two-month trip to India, two years after I started my Jewish journey and ten days after I got engaged.

Four and a half years since the last time I was here, I step out of the airport building to be hit once again by the heat, smell, and noise of Mother India. Immediately swarmed by hopeful taxi drivers and beggars, I take a deep breath, relax, and brace myself for what will surely prove to be another crazy adventure through possibly the most intense and multifaceted place on earth.

An hour later, I get off the still slow-moving local bus in the center of town and step into the stifling, dusty heat and cacophony of car horns that is central Delhi. I start the fifteen-minute walk to Paharganj, the main market area and center of backpacker guesthouses. I used to pride myself on traveling with no more than ten kilograms, but this time I have over twenty, making the walk that much tougher. The sights, sounds, and particularly smells are all so familiar to me, I'm actually almost totally insensitive to it all. Is there such thing as the opposite of culture shock?

I know how to handle the beggars, the rickshaw wallahs,[1] how to dodge the red *paan*[2] spit flying out of people's mouths all over the place.

1 A wallah is a person concerned or involved with a specified thing or business, e.g., "ice cream wallahs."

2 *Paan* is a preparation combining betel leaf with areca nut, and sometimes also tobacco, widely consumed throughout South Asia, Southeast Asia, and Taiwan. It is chewed for its stimulant and psychoactive effects. After chewing, it is either spat out or swallowed.

I am not surprised when the old man walking in front of me veers off to the edge of sidewalk to relieve himself. I nonchalantly avoid motor rickshaws, turn down offers of rides on cycle rickshaws, walk around cows, unfazed by the people lying on the side of the road, maybe dead maybe not.

None of it is new to me. I feel streetwise, an old hand at this solo traveling game. This time, though, I am not searching for truth and meaning, I have already found that. I am not here on holiday, not here for pleasure. I have come with a purpose, a mission to fulfill, and I am going to get it done and get back, as soon as I can, to my *kallah* waiting for me in Jerusalem. I'm here to engage Israeli backpackers in social-justice work with the locals in orphanages and in schools, to share Indian language and culture with them, and to teach them Jewish meditation and spirituality as a counterbalance for those seeking it in Eastern paths. As I walk down the street, the familiar sound of popular mantras is pumped out of shop fronts. Temples in which I once loved meditating now hold no appeal for me. I hang on to my tzitzit and look down at the stripes on my arm left by my tefillin, which I wrapped on the plane as the sun was rising across the plains of India. I find myself singing "*Ki Eshmerah Shabbat*" over and over with a big smile on my face, drowning out the familiar words of the mantras that have returned so vividly to my head.

I arrive at the Namaskar Hotel, where I stayed on my last night in India, four and a half years ago, not a place I would ever take my bride-to-be. I go to the room and immediately fall back into my old routine—shirt off, hang up the mosquito net, check safety in the room (how the door locks, if there is any other way for someone to get in), unpack and reorganize, cold bucket shower to wash off the grime and sweat built up from the second I walked out of the airport building. I saved my kosher breakfast from the plane in case I couldn't find anything to eat. I savor the strawberry yogurt and have a brief nap.

An hour later I awake, sweating, the slow-moving fan turning round monotonously, hardly providing any breeze. I blow my nose and am not surprised when black stuff from all the pollution comes out. I barely look up as a huge cockroach scurries across the room; I just hope it doesn't get to the rest of my kosher food. The old essentials are still here: ten meters of string, Swiss Army knife, mosquito net, padlock, head torch. No huge first aid kit, no injections, no malaria tablets; just Savlon (antiseptic cream) and paracetemol (painkillers)—the cures for all ills.

Yet this time, instead of my reading material being *Autobiography of a Yogi* by Paramahansa Yogananda and *Krishnamurti on Self-awareness*, I am carrying with me a *Chumash*, a siddur, a book on reaching your potential through understanding the energy of the *sefirot*, and *Mesilat Yesharim*, a classic work on personal and spiritual growth.

Now my four-cornered garment has changed from a large woolen Himalayan poncho worn over my clothes to my cotton Jerusalem tzitzit resting underneath my light-blue shirt. Rather than listening to Tibetan mantras and flute music over and over again on a 1980s' Walkman that I bought in the market for two dollars, I have hundreds of *shiurim* and the Moshav Band on my MP3 player.

Equipped very differently and with a very different goal in mind, I'm ready to face the Indian subcontinent once again...

Every year, sixty thousand Israelis go to India, looking for freedom, relaxation, and spirituality after the army. Some will go to a yoga class, classical Indian music lesson, or a hike, some are seriously searching for spirituality and meaning, and in general, people are just chilling out, with no responsibilities and nothing to actually do or achieve. It's like being on a really beautiful, spiritual kibbutz with lots of cheap restaurants and good views. I don't blame them for wanting a break—they totally deserve it. After three years in the army, having been ordered around with no freedom, maybe seeing a friend injured or worse, they just want to get away, treat themselves, and have nothing to think about or do, with no one to tell them how to think, feel, or dress.

Back in my early days in India, I used to hang out with them a lot. Sometimes you could be excused for thinking you were in Israel, hanging out with Israelis, listening to Israeli music, and eating Israeli food, just with the foothills of the Himalayas as the backdrop. They generally follow what has become known as the Hummus Trail; a route of backpacker hotspots not to be missed, including Bhagsu, Manali, Kasol,

Rishikesh, Hampi, and Goa. They were always friendly and interesting, and the ones who had chosen to travel alone, away from the pack, were always among the most special and deep people I met on my travels. In Bhagsu, where I was based, the population is at times 50 percent Israeli. The internet cafés all have Hebrew keyboards, the restaurants sell falafel, hummus, and schnitzel, there are two Chabad Houses and a Lev Yehudi House, and the locals speak decent Hebrew; they have to if they want to make a living.

There's a story about an Indian man who asked an Israeli, "How many Israelis are there?" to which the reply was, "Around seven million." The Indian shook his head and said, "No, no, I meant in Israel, not in India."

Unfortunately, because some Israelis would get out of control and be somewhat lacking in cultural sensitivity, many guesthouses would end up banning Israelis, and travelers from other countries often had their "bad experience with Israelis" story. The main aim of my project was to give Israelis a real taste of India off the hummus trail, teach them Hindi and Indian culture, make sure they were seen to be giving back, and in that way improve to some extent their reputation among the locals. The other aim was to engage in discussions about the Buddhist and Hindu paths they were looking into and show them the depth and beauty of Judaism in contrast.

Just like I had found when I was their age, Western culture wasn't offering what they were looking for, and Judaism, as they perceived it, didn't seem to be the way either. With the societal problems in Israel and the strong religious-secular divide, many of my secular Israeli friends have told me they were brought up to believe that religious people are actually mentally ill. Factors such as these have pushed them to search for spirituality elsewhere, leading them further away from being open to finding out the depth and sweetness of their own heritage. I wanted to show them another side of Judaism: the meditative tradition, the social-justice focus, the personal growth aspects, and help them see past their—often quite understandable—prejudices. It was like a Birthright for Israelis in India, an attempt to show them that everything they were searching for was actually waiting for them at home.

Continued diary entry from when I arrived in Bhagsu looking to set up the program.

I decide to walk off into the mountains to search out local schools and find out what they need and how I can help. On my first foray through the forest and around the mountains, away from the tourist area, I find a school in Bhal Village, with just ten students. Bhal is an hour-and-a-half-trek away from the tourist area, nestled in the side of the mountain, across a spectacular river whose sparkling blue waters rush down through the valley, straight from the snowcapped mountains that form the majestic backdrop. I talk to a local boy who is manning a chai stall and learn that there are a few villages with schools dotted around the mountains. He draws me a simple map, a pencil line, a few villages, a river, scribbled names of places, approximate distances. Just my type of mission. I feel the call of the wild again, arms scratched up from making my way through thorn trees, minimal supplies, not sure what I'll find, where I'll sleep, how long before I return to civilization. All I know is that I have a mission with a defined goal and that it's taking me back, deep into the mountains, into the villages, back to the real India.

This time, however, as with everything since *teshuvah*, it is all so much fuller, clearer, so touched with the Divine. What I once called energy, nature, karma, the universe, is now something much higher—the Creator of energy, nature, karma, and the universe—a Divine Being I can speak to and have a personal relationship with.

Saying *berachot*, almost constant *hitbodedut* as I make my way up and down the steep mountains and along the ridges, singing *niggunim*—in search of the dream. I am now part of a purposeful creation, rather than part of *lila*, the divine sport of the Hindus, or *shunyata*, the emptiness of the Buddhists. As a Jew I am here, not to transcend or disengage from this world, but rather to elevate and perfect it, thereby elevating and perfecting myself.

The stark contrast between this and where I have come from and what I am going back to literally makes me laugh out loud every time I think of it. One month ago, I was studying Talmud in yeshiva, wearing a suit on Shabbat, meeting the foreign ministry to set up my India trip, planning an engagement party. Now I'm scrambling up mountainsides in rolled-up trousers, a sweat-soaked, mud-stained T-shirt, and flip flops in search of *chessed* projects in the foothills of the Himalayas. Totally surreal, both such big parts of who I am.

Nevertheless, whereas once I dreamed of walking off and living this life, surviving in nature, living rough and simply, away from society and civilization, reaching enlightenment in some cave somewhere, or becoming a martial arts master, now the ideas don't excite me anymore. I can't wait to get married, to set up a beautiful Jewish home in Jerusalem, have guests for Shabbat, learn Torah, bring up holy children, set up organizations to help empower other people, dress respectfully to honor Shabbat and festivals. I'll still meditate, go hiking in nature, and train in martial arts, yet as I look at the forty-five-year-old travelers who have never found their place, doomed to wander around trying to impress the backpackers half their age with their travel stories, I am so grateful for having been shown my place, my base, my path, my home, and having been given the person to share it with. Responsibility brings out a new depth in a person.

I have let go of many of my dreams: the three-month canoe trip down the Yukon, the Amazon adventure, shaman training in Mexico, the percussion mission to Ghana. The need to keep going in search of more adventures means you are never at peace, never settled, and what you've found until now never truly satisfied you. It did, however, take something much greater to be able to put those dreams aside, to outshine and replace them, something which I have found in Israel, Torah, and my *kallah*.

I ended up running a couple of trips up into the mountains around Bhagsu, where most of the backpackers never venture, giving them an authentic cultural experience off the beaten track. We schlepped all our cooking equipment and food on our backs, did some pretty grueling climbs up into the mountains, lived rough in small villages, got up early for tai chi and meditation, spent our days teaching in the schools, providing materials and painting the walls, doing music and dance sessions, and would then play music and talk meditation and philosophy deep into the starry night. There were group dynamic issues, personal issues, food issues—all of which strengthened the group, the participants, and the experience as a whole. Most participants shared that it was the most powerful and meaningful experience of their trip to India, giving them a chance to interact authentically with the locals, each other, their Judaism, and themselves. I, too, got so much out of it, being back in the hills, creating projects, and bringing people together, all parts of my life coming together; it felt like my whole journey had been leading to this point. Yet at the same time, my heart and thoughts were often elsewhere, with my *kallah* in Jerusalem and our wedding only seven short weeks away.

I really got the feeling that the time had come for this wandering Jew to finally hang up his backpack and settle down.

Or so I thought...

In 2010, I met Rabbi Jamie Cowland, who set up Justifi, an organization committed to taking Jews from all backgrounds on perspective-shifting adventures to exotic locations around the world. Based on empowering participants to take responsibility for their own well-being and that of the world around them, the trips involve meeting inspirational founders of grassroots organizations, understanding the local culture and the issues they face, doing some hands-on volunteer work, and partaking in meditation and mindfulness sessions in beautiful nature. Since then, I have run dozens of trips to Thailand, Peru, Nicaragua, South Africa, India, and Sri Lanka, where my whole journey began sixteen years ago.

For me, the best thing about the trip is that it brings together a group of Jews from a completely diverse range of backgrounds and Jewish affiliation to do some good and get inspired together. It's awesome to watch people interacting authentically with others they would never usually hang out with or even speak to. Each group learns to drop their prejudices, judgements, and preconceived ideas, and just relate to each other as fellow Jews, usually with similar challenges on their journey through life. Often the best friendships are formed between people from the most dissimilar backgrounds.

It is essential that as a people we start to relate to each other as strongly and healthily as possible. Our strength as a people comes when we are unified, working together in mutual respect. Rabbi Moshe Zeldman asks the question: What connects us as Jews?

It's not religion—some believe, some don't.

It's not race—there are many shades of Jewish people.

It's not that we're a nation—there are Jews of all different countries, languages, and cultures.

So really, what it comes down to is that we are a family, we are B'nei Yisrael—children of Avraham and Sarah, Yitzchak and Rivkah, Yaakov, Leah, and Rachel.

What I find so sad is that yes, we are a family, but often we seem like a pretty dysfunctional one. Our radically different beliefs and lifestyles can push us toward distrust and confrontation, yet it is crucial that we find some way to love each other despite the differences. The greater the Jewish leader, the greater their love was for all Jews, no matter what their background and belief system.

The Torah[3] teaches "ואהבת לרעך כמוך—love your fellow as yourself." That does not exclude those who believe and practice differently from us; in fact, quite the opposite—it is *davka* these relationships the Torah is asking us to work on. As I shared before, my *rebbeim* always said to me that the more connected I become to Hashem, the less judgmental and more open and loving I should be becoming. If the opposite happens, I didn't become religious, I became self-righteous.

The Justifi trips are an equalizer. It doesn't matter what background you are from; learning about atrocities happening around the world is shocking. It doesn't matter what your affiliation; we all need time to disconnect from the Internet and work and reconnect to ourselves. It doesn't matter where you come from; playing with elephants in a sanctuary and zip-lining through the forests is truly thrilling. When we can start to find common goals and common ground, working to see the

3 *Vayikra* 19:18.

good in each other, we can start to rebuild our people and go a long way to reaching our national destiny.

One morning on our trip to Sri Lanka, I was davening *Shacharit* as the sun was rising over the enchanting forested city of Kandy. Suddenly, over the loudspeakers from the temples in the city below came the familiar chanting as the monks started up their morning spiritual routine. I smiled as I fondly remembered my days chanting those morning precepts, working on overcoming ego and craving. Yet more than that, I felt grateful that my morning chants had turned from focusing on non-self and emptiness into *Pesukei d'Zimra*, songs of praise and prayer, directed at a relationship with the Divine Presence pervading Creation. From trips in India with Israeli backpackers, to Thailand and Sri Lanka with American students and young professionals, it's truly exceptional for me to be back in my old hunting grounds where everything is so familiar, seeing where my path has taken me and reaching out to my brothers and sisters to offer them some support and insights on their own journey.

I reveled in the fact that I'd come full circle—but couldn't have been in a more different place.

I reveled in the fact that I'd come full circle—but couldn't have been in a more different place.

CHAPTER 14

The Continuing Journey to Jewish Enlightenment

Man cannot rely on intellect alone to determine his spiritual work. A connection based on intellect alone is not long-lasting. He can know intellectually...yet his heart and body remain far behind. He needs to bind his whole soul and life force [to Hashem] and penetrate his soul to elevate and awaken it, so it becomes passionate about all mitzvot, about Torah and tefillah, and find true spiritual delight and joy in them.

Piaseczno Rav, Chovot HaTalmidim

Eleven years after arriving in Israel, I am now blessed to be working at Aish HaTorah in Jerusalem, where I spend all day interacting with Jewish people of all ages and diverse backgrounds—the unaffiliated, the observant, people who were observant and now aren't, people who weren't observant and are moving in that direction—all searching for something more in life. It is truly heartening to see so many Jews returning to their tradition, finding depth, meaning, truth, and joy through the Torah.

Rav Noach Weinberg used to put the proposition as follows: Say you have a billionaire uncle and he died and left you an envelope. He wasn't your closest relative and didn't necessarily seem like the greatest person in the world, but he left you this envelope nonetheless. Would you go and collect it? Maybe there'll be nothing inside, maybe just twenty dollars, but you never know, you might hit the jackpot. Either way, it's definitely worth taking the time to check it out.

Judaism makes the claim that it has access to the word of the Divine Creator, that it has the evidence to support this claim, and that it is the Guidebook toward living the best life possible. Yes, following the path does mean some sacrifices, yet if the claim is true, the things we need to sacrifice aren't in our best interest anyway.

It's incredibly empowering and inspiring being in an environment where people are grappling for the truth, facing themselves and reality every day, and striving to reach their potential. I wake up every morning feeling that I am actually living the whole purpose of life: striving to become a *tzaddik*, forming the deepest, most authentic relationship with Hashem possible, as well as guiding others toward doing the same thing.

On the other hand, it hurts me so much to see how many Jewish kids from around the world are leaving their Jewish identities behind. Many of these come from nonobservant homes where they were never really given any reason to "stay Jewish"; many others grew up in observant homes, but something went wrong in their Jewish education or their social or family life, or the lure of the secular world was just too strong. I speak to many kids who were brought up with a Judaism that was less than warm and inspiring, where they were just told by well-meaning teachers and parents to do things, without really understanding the depth and meaning behind them. They often tell me they grew up with the idea that Hashem is an angry man in the sky and we have to do what He says or He will punish us. It's hard to build a close personal relationship with a G-d like that. Halachah can seem restrictive and davening impersonal. Some started questioning things as they got older and came into contact with secular ideas and science, and the adults they asked were unequipped with the knowledge, evidence, or understanding to answer their questions. They often leave the path because the path they were shown was unable to offer them what their minds and souls were yearning for. If only they were shown the true depth and beauty of Judaism, they'd never have felt let down. In fact, we are facing somewhat of a crisis as many more people are leaving Yiddishkeit than returning, intermarriage rates are extremely high, many religious Jews feel that they are just going through the motions, some *baalei teshuvah* run out of steam five years down the road, and many Jews don't even identify as being Jewish anymore.

Looking into Judaism from the outside as I did for the first twenty-nine years of my life, I wasn't too impressed either.

On one hand it was because of my own shortcomings. I realized that even though I had a strong Jewish identity, went to Hebrew school, had a bar mitzvah and Friday night dinners, celebrated the festivals, played on a Jewish football team, visited Israel, and had mostly Jewish friends, I was basically totally uneducated when it came to what the Torah actually teaches and why we believe that to be true. I had a superficial understanding of the beliefs and the rituals and was easily put off by things I saw in the Torah that went against my Western secular moral value system. I had never interacted with religious Jews, happy to just judge them unfavorably from afar. In short, I was uninformed and assumed things about the religion and its adherents without really challenging myself to look a little deeper.

On the other hand, it was because of some shortcomings I observed, and am still faced with in the Orthodox community today. It's amazing how many conversations I have with highly conscious, spiritually seeking Jews who come into Aish and want to know why, if the Torah is true and enlightening, there is not more emphasis on issues such as physical health, protecting the environment, universalism, and an appreciation of art, music, and culture within the religious community.

The truth is that Judaism *is* a holistic path to perfecting ourselves and the world around us. The Rambam speaks of exercise and healthy eating as prerequisites for spiritual connection,[1] and the Torah and Midrash urges us to be environmentally conscious. As far as other nations are concerned, the Midrash tells us that there is great wisdom among them,[2]

---

1 *Hilchot De'ot* 4.

2 *Eichah Rabbah* 2:13.

and *Tanna D'Vei Eliyahu Rabbah*[3] teaches that *ruach ha'kodesh*, the holy spirit, rests on man, woman, Jew, and non-Jew, according to their deeds.

So when asked about this, I acknowledge their point and admit that religious Jews are just as human as everyone else, having their shortcomings, challenges, and areas they need to work on. Being religious doesn't automatically make someone happy and perfect; we all have personal and societal struggles to overcome and have to prioritize which areas of growth to work on. There are also some times when people who are dressed as religious Jews can behave in ways that give the religion a bad name, but they aren't representative of the religion at all—in fact, it's only when they are going against Torah that the negativity comes out. However, I then feel compelled to point out that as a whole, I have found that there is more goodwill, strength in community, welcoming of guests, giving of tzedakah, sense of purpose, focus on growth, learning, and the development and teaching of good values and character traits than in any other community I have ever come across anywhere in the world. The amount of charitable organizations, leadership and growth initiatives, and learning opportunities is truly remarkable.

Yet we do seem to be facing one real issue, one that Rav Soloveitchik expresses in his usual clear and insightful manner:

> *Contemporary Orthodoxy is well-grounded intellectually. In spite of this, its followers lack passion and enthusiasm...from within the allegedly dry confines of Jewish law, there is an awesome, warm, enormous world—there is a definite transition from halachah to service of Hashem."*[4]

Notwithstanding some issues of philosophy and practice, when one walks into a Buddhist Temple in Thailand, you feel an aura of peace and serenity, removed from the hustle and bustle of everyday life. Step into

---

3 *Tanna D'Vei Eliyahu Rabbah* 9:
פנחס בן אלעזר היה בימים ההם מעיד אני עלי את השמים ואת הארץ בין ישראל בין עכו"ם בין איש בין אשה בין עבד ובין שפחה הכל לפי המעשה שהוא עושה כך רוח הקודש שורה עליו.

4 *Before Hashem You Will Be Purified: Rabbi Joseph B. Soloveitchik on the Days of Awe*, summarized and annotated by Arnold Lustiger (1998).

a Hindu Temple in India and you are met with a profound sense of the heightened spiritual energy pervading the atmosphere. Unfortunately, the same doesn't always seem to be the case when you walk into a synagogue. It can feel like, as Rav Soleveitchik continues, "many Jews don't want to pray, they want to *have* prayed."

There are so many really nice, good, *frum* people, who keep kosher and Shabbat and all the mitzvot, whose kids go to yeshiva, who learn Torah, and dress modestly. All this is crucial—it's who we are and what we need to do and it's keeping Judaism alive. Yet sometimes it seems like people lose the center and purpose of it all: a truly intimate, authentic, personal relationship with themselves and Hashem. Sometimes it feels like we have the body of Jewish practice, we're just lacking the heart. As the Ramchal laments in the introduction to *Mesilat Yesharim*:

> *There are those who have entered the realm of the sacred and are studying the Holy Torah...however, few among them choose to devote thought and study to the total perfection of the Divine service—ahavah, yirah, deveikut, and all other aspects of piety...which is the very essence of what Hashem is asking of us!*[5]

The truth is that just being *yotzei*, ticking the boxes, and going through the motions is not the goal. Doing our religious obligations quickly so we can get back to the work or entertainment that we value more is not the way it's meant to be. We were created with the express purpose of reidentifying ourselves as souls, feeling close to Hashem in a palpable way, and bringing G-d-consciousness into the world. The Torah and halachah are the guidelines, leading us toward an experience. It's easy to get caught up in the laws and lose sight of the destination.

Rabbi David Aaron compares it to just looking at a menu in a restaurant without actually tasting the food or studying the maps without going on the beautiful hike. Or, as one of my first teachers said, "It is

5 Introduction to *Mesilat Yesharim*:
אחרים יכנסו יותר אל הקדש, דהיינו, למוד התורה הקדושה אך מעטים יהיו מן המין הזה אשר יקבעו עיון ולמוד על עניני שלמות העבודה, על האהבה, על היראה, על הדבקות, ועל כל שאר חלקי החסידות.

like a finger pointing away to the moon; don't concentrate on that finger or you will miss all the heavenly glory."[6]

We could be learning Torah and davening all day, working on our character traits, and doing mitzvot, yet be sadly missing what it is all for. Torah is a Guidebook leading us to an experience. Just studying the Guidebook without tasting the experience means we could miss the whole point.

> *A story is told of the Chiddushei HaRim, who was walking with a student and told him that one day there will be a time when there'll be a proliferation of yeshivas, study halls, Torah literature, Jewish organizations and shuls, tzedakah and mitzvot. Yet at that time there'll be one thing missing: Hashem.*

So what is the *avodah* we need to be implementing in our lives? The Talmud teaches that "רחמנא ליבא בעי—the Compassionate One just wants the heart."[7] He wants us to really mean what we do, to do things consciously and build a real, deep, loving, authentic relationship. The *Shulchan Aruch*[8] teaches that less done with more intention is better than doing a lot without intention, and the *Mishnah Berurah* adds that "one can do a lot, one can do a little, just as long as the heart is directed toward Heaven."[9]

Mesilat Yesharim teaches:

> *The Master Blessed Be He is not satisfied with deeds alone in the performance of mitzvot. Rather, what is most important to Him is that the heart be so pure that it directs itself to true service of the eternal.*[10]

It all comes down to a question of whether our heart is truly in it, and if we really mean and feel it. We say in *Aleinu* three times a day:

---

6 Bruce Lee in *Enter the Dragon*.

7 *Sanhedrin* 106a.

8 *Shulchan Aruch, Orach Chaim* 1:4.

9 *Orach Chaim* 1:4:12: אחד המרבי ואחד הממעיט ובלבד שיכון לבו לשמים.

10 Chapter on "Holiness":
כי אין די לאדון ברוך הוא במעשים לבדם שיהיו מעשי מצוה, אלא העיקר לפניו שהלב יהיה טהור לכוין בה לעבודה אמיתית.

וידעת היום והשבת אל לבבך כי ה׳ הוא האלקים בשמים ממעל ועל הארץ מתחת אין עוד:

And we should know today and place it in our heart that Hashem is our G-d in the heavens above and on the earth below, there is nothing else.[11]

Just knowing, even an intimate knowing, is not enough.[12] It needs to be settled into and make an impression on our heart. One day just before Shavuot, I was saying this passage when I noticed it contains the words *daat* (knowledge) and *yishuv* (to settle). It is teaching us the need to "settle the knowledge" in our hearts. This called to mind a famous teaching in *Likutei Moharan*, where Rebbe Nachman teaches us that

מה שהעולם רחוקים מהשם יתברך ואינם מתקרבים אליו יתברך הוא רק מחמת שאין להם ישוב הדעת.

The reason the world feels far from Hashem and is not coming close to Him, may He be blessed, is only because they have no yishuv ha'daat—settling (or peace) of mind.[13]

Putting these two teachings together, it occurred to me that *yishuv ha'daat* means on the one hand to settle our minds down and find peace and clarity, while on the other, it also expresses the real goal of this exercise, which is to "*yishuv* the *daat*," to settle the intimate knowledge into our hearts and live fully with it. Once our mind is calm and still, we clear up space to feel the innate connection we already have in our heart and soul. *Pirkei Avot* teaches:

Go and see which is the best trait for a person to acquire. Said Rabbi Eliezer: A good eye. Said Rabbi Yehoshua: A good friend. Said Rabbi Yossi: A good neighbor. Said Rabbi

---

11 *Devarim* 4:39.

12 *Daat* implies an intimate knowledge. The Torah (*Bereishit* 4:1) tells us that "והאדם ידע את חוה אשתו—Adam *knew* his wife Chavah."

13 *Likutei Moharan, Tinyana* 10.

> *Shimon: To see what is born [out of one's actions]. Said Rabbi Elazar: A good heart. Said he (Rav Yochanan) to them: I prefer the words of Elazar the son of Arach to yours, for his words include all of yours.*[14]

A true Enlightened Jewish Master is one who compliments his balanced, trained, and healthy mind with a pure, good, and open heart.

The most essential and powerful practice we need to bring our hearts into the picture is what the Talmud calls *avodah she'ba'lev*, the work of the heart.

> איזו היא עבודה שהיא בלב? הוי אומר זו תפלה.
>
> *What is the service of the heart? It is tefillah—prayer.*[15]

Prayer itself should come from the heart, and we use it as a time to ask Hashem for help in purifying our hearts to be able to connect to Him even more authentically.

> לב טהור ברא לי אלוקים ורוח נכון חדש בקרבי:
>
> *G-d, create for me a pure heart, and renew the correct spirit within me.*[16]

> וטהר לבנו לעבדך באמת.
>
> *Purify our hearts to serve You in truth.*[17]

What this points to is that the most powerful way to build a real, authentic, intimate relationship with Hashem is though speaking to Him honestly and openly from the heart. Jewish prayer isn't an attempt to connect to a separate Being, thanking and praising and requesting things from Him. Rather, the word for prayer—להתפלל—is reflexive, i.e., something we are doing to ourselves! Various interpretations teach

---

14 *Avot* 2:10.

15 *Taanit* 2a.

16 *Tehillim* 51:12.

17 Shabbat davening.

that we are evaluating ourselves,[18] connecting to ourselves,[19] and envisioning the ultimate state of our lives and the world.[20] To pray is the ultimate expression of our souls.

Rav Moshe Weinberger teaches that our connection to our souls, Yiddishkeit, and Hashem can be on one of the four levels of life on this earth: דומם—inanimate, צומח—vegetable, חי—animal, and מדבר—human. For some people it is *domem*, quiet[21] and stagnant like a rock. Then there are those who are *tzomei'ach*, growing, beginning to be aroused to seek more depth, more meaning, and more connection. Above that there are those who are *chai*, truly living with this consciousness, getting up to daven, learning, doing mitzvot, and working on themselves.

Yet there is a level even higher than this. Rav Weinberger points out that the word for human is *medaber*, "one who speaks." The highest level of connection to self, Yiddishkeit, and Hashem is to be in a constant conversation with Him, to open our hearts and speak directly to Him, like a best friend, twin, father, guide, and even spouse. The Torah tells us that Hashem gave Adam a soul, at which point he became a *nefesh chayah*, translated by Onkelos as a speaking spirit. Rav Elimelech Biderman points out that when he was created, Adam was alone, with no one to talk to. This must mean that he was created to speak to Hashem![22]

Try out this essential Enlightened Jewish Master authentic connection exercise.

Find at least five minutes a day to sit and speak to Hashem authentically from your heart. (Separate from formal prayer times.)

- Your phone should be far away from you.
- Speak in whatever language you feel most comfortable expressing yourself.

---

18 *Berachot* 26b; *Tehillim* 106:30.

19 Rashi, *Bereishit* 30:8, *Parashat Vayetzei*.

20 Ibid., 48:11, *Parashat Vayechi*.

21 *Domem* is related to the word דממה, silence, as in קול דְּמָמָה דַקָּה (I *Melachim* 19:12).

22 *Torah Wellsprings*, *Parashat Noach* 5779.

- It can't just be thoughts—the words have to leave your lips and you should be able to hear them.
- The more solitary a place you can find, the better. Nature is good, but really you could do this anywhere.[23]
- You can talk about anything—how your day was, what you are struggling with, what you're grateful for, what you are yearning for. The key is just to be real. If you feel strange doing this exercise, tell Him that. If you are doubting Him or yourself, tell Him that. If you can't think of something to say, sing a *niggun*. It doesn't matter what happens—just have a date with Hashem for at least five minutes a day.

We must realize that with all the ideas and exercises in the book, it's only by asking for *siyata d'Shmaya*, Divine assistance, that we will be able to succeed. The truth is that in all the areas we've discussed in each chapter—gratitude, correcting character traits, building self-esteem, and self-control—the primary *hishtadlut* (effort), as the Ramchal says,[24] is to speak to Hashem about it.

23 I once couldn't find a private place, so I leaned against the wall and pretended I was talking on my phone to someone.

24 *Derech Hashem* 4:5:2.

Epilogue

Life is a great battle. Our adversary, the *yetzer hara*, is always ready to pounce; it knows us intimately, has many tactics, and never gives up.[1] Our masters have revealed to us the key factor we need in order to fight and beat the *yetzer hara*. In *Parashat Bereishit*, when Hashem didn't accept Kayin's offering, Kayin got very disheartened.[2] Hashem reassured him that he could always do better next time, and warned him that the *yetzer hara* is always ready to attack, but it is possible to conquer it.

On this idea—that we can conquer our *yetzer hara*—Rashi says just four words: "אם תרצה תתגבר עליו—If you want to, you will beat it."[3] Incredible! All we need is to really *want* to beat it. Once we have a strong enough *ratzon* to beat it, a strong enough desire and yearning to be *tzaddikim*, nothing can get in our way.

The Torah[4] teaches us that these things are not far from us, not in heaven and not across the sea. They are very near to us—in our hearts! It has all been placed in front of us, and at this point we just need to choose it! David HaMelech says in *Tehillim*,[5] "כאיל תערוג על אפיקי מים כן נפשי תערוג אליך אלקים." This is usually translated as, "Like a deer yearns for brooks of water, so too my soul is yearning for You, my G-d." Yet a closer look reveals that David used the word על, which means "on." The deer is *on* the water—he is right there already! He just needs to open his eyes and his heart to reveal it. *Mesilat Yesharim* sums up for us what it really takes to become true Enlightened Jewish Masters:

---

1 See *Chovot HaLevavot*, chap. 5.

2 *Bereishit*, chap. 4.

3 Ibid., 4:7.

4 *Devarim* 30:11–20, *Parashat Nitzavim*.

5 *Tehillim* 42:2.

> *Anything he sees that is a way to draw close to Hashem, he will chase after it, grab hold of it, and not let it go. And anything that he sees as an obstacle to this, he should flee from it as one flees from fire. For his coming to this world is only for this purpose, namely, to attain this closeness…*

We are all writing and illustrating the story of our lives, moment by moment, and one day we will look back and, hopefully, enjoy reading what we wrote. We just need to ask ourselves the big questions: What are we living for? What are we yearning for? What are we investing our time, money, effort, emotion, heart, and soul into? Do we fall asleep thinking about our business, our worries, or about becoming *tzaddikim*? Are we more concerned about looking and feeling good, or being and doing good? What is going to bring us the most depth, growth, meaning, and joy in life?

Once we've clarified our destination and identified the path to reach it, all we need to do is put in the effort to move with passion and determination in that direction, enjoying the adventure as we go. That way we'll end our lives with no regrets, having climbed the mountains, surfed the waves, traversed the deserts, survived the falls, and scaled the heights, as we walk the holy path of the Enlightened Jewish Master.

> *And if he is a true master and triumphs in the war from all sides, he will become the perfect person, and merit to cleave fully to the Creator. He will leave the training ground and enter into the palace, permeated with the glow of life. And to the degree he succeeded in conquering his negative thoughts and desires, distanced himself from things that take him far away from the great goodness, and strove to connect to Him, so he will attain his goal and find true joy!*[6]

We should all be blessed with deep connection to Hashem, ourselves, our families, all the Yidden, and the whole *briah*.

---

6 *Mesilat Yesharim*, chap. 1:
ואם יהיה לבן חיל וינצח המלחמה מכל הצדדין, הוא יהיה האדם השלם אשר יזכה לידבק בבוראו ויצא מן הפרוזדור הזה ויכנס בטרקלין לאור באור החיים. וכפי השיעור אשר כבש את יצרו ותאוותיו ונתרחק מן המרחיקים אותו מהטוב ונשתדל לדבק בו, כן ישיגהו וישמח בו.

Postscript

On September 28th, 2018, which was Friday night of Sukkot, my wife's waters broke, and we rushed to Shaarei Tzedek hospital in an ambulance. The reason we rushed rather than calmly packed up our stuff and made our way to the hospital was because the baby's due date was actually January 12th 2019—more than three months later.

After two weeks of bedrest, our son was born on October 14th, the fifth of Cheshvan, at twenty-seven weeks, weighing just over one kilogram.

The first time I saw him, apart from a brief glimpse as he was whisked past me in an incubator straight from the operating room, was an hour after the birth, in the *pagiyah*, the Neonatal Intensive Care Unit (NICU), which was to be his (and our) home for the next three months. (I slept in the family room near the NICU almost every night until he was released.)

We were faced with what was clearly a displaced fetus rather the usual newborn. He was literally being kept alive with the help of an incubator (which I called the incu-Beit Hamikdash), a respirator, a feeding tube up his nose, something in his abdomen, and several wires connecting him to an array of beeping monitors. Many flashing lights were constantly signaling his oxygen, pulse, and blood pressure rates, and we soon got used to the various beeps and buzzes, learning which ones to ignore and which ones would bring the nurses running.

Over the next three months, the process of growing our baby outside the womb included many milestones—holding him for the first time (on his third day), watching him come off the respirator, dressing him in clothing, moving him from an incubator into a heated half-incubator, leaving the intensive care ward into the "not-so-intensive" care ward, seeing him come off the oxygen, feeding him from a bottle—as well as many set-backs. Before we were allowed to take him home, he was back on the respirator, suffered stomach infections, received blood transfusions, was back on the feeding tube, and had hernias. And then, in order to bring him home, we had to learn preemie CPR.

I often say that my goal is to be a *tzaddik* by the time I'm ninety. After going through this, I think I could make it by eighty-nine. Here are some (of the many) insights I had during this time, which will hopefully help you deal with your challenges in life.

BARUCH HASHEM, from the moment our son was born, Hashem gave me the presence of mind to know with certainty that it would all be fine in the end, and that even if on the surface it seemed to turn out not so fine, the end result would clearly be what we needed in our life to help us reach our goals of *emunah*, self-perfection, and closeness to Hashem. In fact, the biggest thing I was afraid of was coming out on the other side of the ordeal without being a significantly different and more refined person, closer to Hashem and propelled toward my goal.

Every challenge is an opportunity to grow, a call from Hashem to step up and come closer—and the bigger the challenge, the bigger the growth opportunity. By living with the truths that *gam zu l'tovah*, this too is for the good,[7] and that *kol mah d'avid Rachmana l'tav avid*, everything the Compassionate One does He does for the good,[8] we can face every challenge with clarity and calm. Instead of asking "why me," "what if," or "if only," we can ask ourselves (and Hashem) what we need to do and get from the situation we are in.

At one point, around two months in, I was feeling pretty exhausted from working all day and being in the hospital all night, dealing with the kids at home, some financial issues, a broken computer, and a bike with a flat tire. When one more thing happened (I couldn't find my keys or the kids were fighting, or something like that), I found myself

7 *Taanit* 21a

8 *Berachot* 60b. The *Shulchan Aruch* (230:5) actually teaches as halachah that we should regularly say this!

saying, "Hashem, please, I really don't need this right now!" Yet, as soon as that thought entered my mind, a huge grin came to my face. Why? Because we know that if "this" is happening—whatever "this" is—then we clearly *do* need this right now! It is exactly what we need!

This gave me a new insight into the blessing we make each morning—*She'asa li kol tzarki*, Who gives me everything I need. It doesn't just mean that He gives me the food, clothes, family, and good things I need, but rather that everything He gives me, even the seemingly "bad" things, are exactly what I need!

This realization doesn't negate the fact that an experience may be painful and difficult nor the possibility of crying out to Hashem for help—in fact, that might be the very reason He's putting us through it, to call out and come closer to Him—it just means we can let go of the complaining, worrying, anger, guilt, and doubt that do nothing to help the situation, and instead, we can focus on what needs to be done.

As I watched our baby's tiny chest being forced up and down by the respirator (since his brain wasn't developed enough to tell his lungs to work, and his lungs weren't developed enough to work anyway), it hit me powerfully that we are all being kept alive at every moment by being connected to the Divine Respirator, who is pumping life and breath into us at every second. Just like we aren't beating our heart, so too, most of the time we are not breathing—we are *being* breathed.

My breathing meditation became much more powerful; instead of controlling my breaths, I just watched myself being breathed, kept alive moment by moment by the Divine force behind all existence. This is a powerful tool to fully experience being alive, being a soul. By just taking time to focus on our breath, we can have the most intimate feeling of our essential connection to Hashem and draw our peace of mind and vitality in life directly from that.

EVENTUALLY, on January 9th, 2019, just as suddenly as it all began, and three days before his due date, we got a call from the NICU telling us not to forget to bring a car seat, as our baby was being released that day. We could have done with some warning, but we weren't complaining. In the end, he left the womb on *Parashat Lech Lecha* (Go) and came home on *Parashat Bo* (Come).

A week after he was born, I told my wife that I feel bad for most people. They take their kids home after two days and have a *bris* six days later. That's certainly very special, but they never get to experience the power of the *bris* we were anticipating, after having invested three months into getting our baby there! And so it was, on Monday, January 14th, exactly three months after he was born, our baby finally joined the covenant of his forefathers and received his name, Avraham Shimshon Elimelech.

Zeh ha'katan gadol yihiye, this little one should become big/great!—and so too, we should all make sure that we keep growing, leaving our *katnut* and achieving true *gadlut*. Amen.[9]

---

9 For more insights and stories, go to www.soundcloud.com/dov-ber-cohen/hayeled-ben-oriana-devorah, and for the short video I made for the *bris*, see www.youtube.com/watch?v=QqPy-x8O7vc&t=1s.

APPENDIX

Sample Cheshbon HaNefesh Chart

BECOMING A TZADDIK—ENLIGHTENED JEWISH MASTER

First, define the goal for yourself; for example, working on becoming a *tzaddik*. A *tzaddik* (or *tzaddikah*) is someone who has perfected his (or her) thoughts, speech, and actions and is living with an authentic, conscious, and joyful personal relationship with Hashem based on the Torah, while helping others do the same. Then, choose areas to work on and set goals. For example:

Wake-up	*latest 7:00 AM, Modeh Ani with kavanah, negel vasser by the bed, neitz once a week*
Davening	*arrive early, first berachah of Shemoneh Esrei extra kavanah, Ashrei and Aleinu from siddur*
Health	*ten minutes stretching a day, no white sugar, green tea instead of coffee, ten push-ups*
Shalom bayit	*date once a week, gift every two weeks, don't leave socks lying around, call often*
Middot	*notice jealous thoughts—smile and replace, two acts of chessed a day*
Torah	*at least two hours a day, fifteen minutes mussar a day, take notes, schmooze less*

My ratings (I have used Hebrew terms here to represent a scale of one to five):

Sunday	Tzaddik	Mensch	Yotzei	Am Ha'aretz
Wake-up				
Davening				
Health				
Shalom bayit				
Middot				
Torah				

Monday	Tzaddik	Mensch	Yotzei	Am Ha'aretz
Wake-up				
Davening				
Health				
Shalom bayit				
Middot				
Torah				

Tuesday	Tzaddik	Mensch	Yotzei	Am Ha'aretz
Wake-up				
Davening				
Health				
Shalom bayit				
Middot				
Torah				

Wednesday	Tzaddik	Mensch	Yotzei	Am Ha'aretz
Wake-up				
Davening				
Health				
Shalom bayit				
Middot				
Torah				

Thursday	Tzaddik	Mensch	Yotzei	Am Ha'aretz
Wake-up				
Davening				
Health				
Shalom bayit				
Middot				
Torah				

Friday	Tzaddik	Mensch	Yotzei	Am Ha'aretz
Wake-up				
Davening				
Health				
Shalom bayit				
Middot				
Torah				

Comments/Need to work on/Need to do teshuvah for:

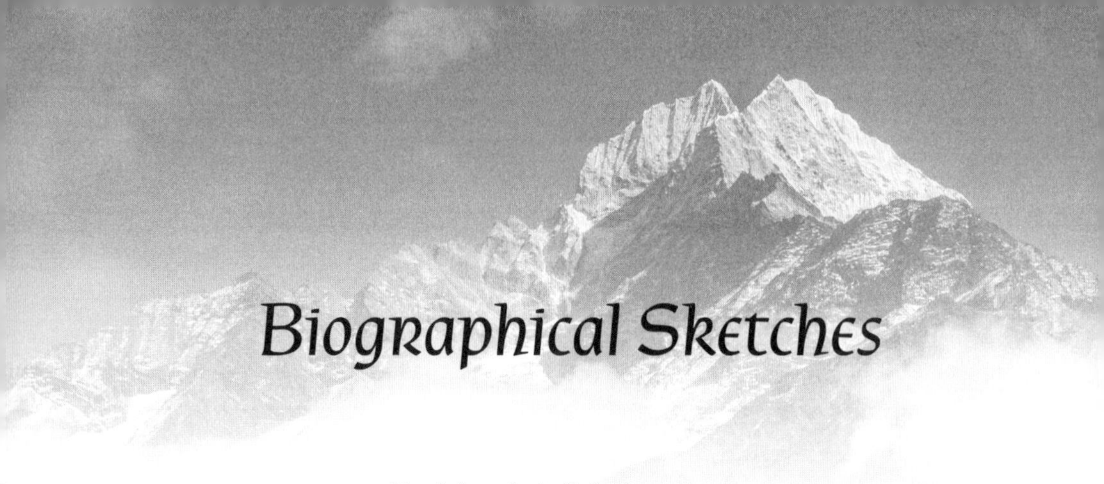

Biographical Sketches

Listed chronologically by date of passing

Hillel the Elder (110 BCE–10 CE) was one of the most important figures in Jewish history. He is associated with the development of the Mishnah and the Talmud. He was born in Babylon, and later moved to Jerusalem during the time of King Herod.

Rabbi Shimon bar Yochai (80–160), also known as **Rashbi**, was a prominent Tannaic (Mishnaic) sage who lived in Israel after the destruction of the Second Temple. He authored the *Zohar*, a foundational work of Kabbalah. He is buried in Meron in northern Israel.

Rabbi Shlomo Yitzchaki (1040–1105), known as **Rashi**, was (and still is) the foremost commentator on the Tanach and Talmud. His commentary is studied by everyone from children to the greatest rabbis of the generation. No Talmud was ever printed without his commentary, and several great Rabbis wrote commentaries on his commentaries. He was born and he died in Troyes in northern France.

Rabbi Moshe ben Maimon; Maimonides (1135–1204), also known as the **Rambam**, was one of the leading Torah scholars and Jewish philosophers of the Middle Ages. He lived in Cairo, Egypt. He famously authored the fourteen-volume *Mishneh Torah*—a comprehensive code to Jewish law—as well as the *Moreh Nevuchim* (Guide for the Perplexed).

Rabbi Moses ben Nachman (1194–1270), also known as **Nachmanides**, was a leading medieval Jewish scholar, Sephardic rabbi, philosopher, physician, kabbalist, and biblical commentator. He is also considered to be an important figure in the re-establishment of the Jewish community in Jerusalem following its destruction by the Crusaders in 1099.

Rabbi Isaac Luria (1534–1572), commonly known as the **Arizal**, was a famous rabbi and Kabbalist who lived and is buried in Tsfat, Israel. He is considered the father of contemporary Kabbalah, and his teachings are known as Lurianic Kabbalah.

Rabbi Moshe Chaim Luzzatto (1707–1746), also known as the **Ramchal**, was a prominent Italian Jewish rabbi, Kabbalist, and philosopher. His most famous works include *Mesilat Yesharim* (The Path of the Just) and *Derech Hashem* (The Way of God). He is buried in Tiberias.

The Baal Shem Tov (1698–1760), Rabbi Israel ben Eliezer, was a mystical rabbi and the founder of Chassidic Judaism. His teachings were based upon the Kabbalah and were aimed at infusing even unlearned Jews with joy and authentic connection in their relationship with Hashem. He is buried in Medzibuz, Ukraine.

Rabbi Elimelech of Lizhensk (1717–1786) was one of the great Chassidic *rebbes* of the eighteenth century and student of the Maggid of Mezeritch—the successor to the Baal Shem Tov. He authored the *Book for Tzaddikim—Noam Elimelech.*

Rabbi Eliyahu ben Shlomo Zalman (1720–1797), commonly known as the **Vilna Gaon**, was one of the greatest Jewish scholars, whose knowledge of every aspect of Torah learning was unparalleled. He was the acknowledged leader of non-Chassidic Jewry in Eastern Europe.

Rabbi Zusha of Hanipol (1718–1800) was one of the great Chassidic *rebbes* of the eighteenth century and a student of the Maggid of Mezeritch—the successor to the Baal Shem Tov. He and his brother, of Rabbi Elimelech of Lizhensk, are both central figures in Chassidic Judaism.

Rabbi Nachman of Breslov (1772–1810) was the great-grandson of the Baal Shem Tov and a famous Chassidic teacher. He is the founder of the Breslov Chassidic movement and author of *Likutei Moharan*. He is buried in Uman, Ukraine.

Rabbi Akiva Eiger (1761–1837) was an outstanding Talmudic scholar, hugely influential in matters of Jewish law, and foremost leader of

European Jewry during the early nineteenth century. He is buried in Poznan, Poland.

Rabbi Menachem Mendel of Kotzk (1787–1859), known as the **Kotzke Rebbe**, was a Chassidic master in Poland. A great Talmudist and Kabbalist, he was famous for his direct path, authenticity, and unwavering devotion to living with the truth.

Rabbi Yitzchak Meir Rothenberg Alter (1799–1866), also known as the **Chiddushei HaRim**, was the founder and first *rebbe* of the Gerrer Chassidic dynasty, which to this day remains one of the largest Chassidic groups. He wrote the *Chiddushei HaRim*, which was a commentary Talmud and *Shulchan Aruch* (Code of Jewish Law).

Rabbi Yisrael Meir HaKohen (1838–1933), commonly known as the **Chofetz Chaim**, was an influential rabbi of the Mussar movement, expert in Jewish law, and ethicist, whose works continue to be widely influential in Jewish life. His most famous work was the *Mishnah Berurah*—a comprehensive commentary on the *Shulchan Aruch* (Code of Jewish Law). He lived in Belarus.

Rabbi Avraham Yitzchak HaCohen Kook (1865–1935) was the first Ashkenazic Chief Rabbi of pre-state Israel and a great Kabbalist and Torah scholar. He is considered one of the fathers of Religious Zionism.

Rabbi Kalonymus Kalman Shapira (1889–1943), known as the **Piaseczna Rebbe**, wrote several books on the Jewish path of personal growth, connecting to Torah and educating children. He is best known for his book *Aish Kodesh* that was written while he was interned in the Warsaw Ghetto—where he fought to keep Jewish life vibrant and uplift the souls and strengthen the faith of those suffering the traumas of the war. He buried the book in a cannister, which was found after the war. He was eventually murdered by the Nazis at a labor camp in 1943.

Rabbi Moshe Feinstein (1895–1986) was a leading adjudicator of questions related to Jewish law and was regarded by most as the authoritative standard for all observant Jews in North America.

Rabbi Joseph B. Soloveitchik (1903–1993) was a major American Orthodox rabbi, Talmudist, and modern Jewish philosopher. He served as an advisor, guide, mentor, and role model for tens of thousands of Jews, both as a Talmudic scholar and as a religious leader. He is regarded as a highly important figure by Modern Orthodox Judaism.

Rabbi Menachem Mendel Schneerson (1902–1994), also known as the **Lubavitcher Rebbe**, was a Russian Empire–born American Orthodox Jewish rabbi, and the last *rebbe* of the Lubavitcher Chassidic dynasty.

Rabbi Noach Weinberg (1930–2009) was a pioneer of the Kiruv movement, reaching out to engage Jews who had little Jewish identity, knowledge, and background. In 1974, he established Aish HaTorah in the Old City of Jerusalem with five students. Aish now has over thirty branches worldwide, and the Jerusalem World Center runs programming for over a hundred thousand people a year.

About the Author

After spending six years living in Asia, learning and teaching Eastern religions and martial arts, as well as spending time volunteering in orphanages, Dov Ber moved to Israel, where he discovered the depth, beauty, truth, and wisdom of Judaism. He made aliyah and, alongside learning in yeshiva, set up his social justice organization, All for the Kids, which raised money and awareness for orphanages in India, Africa, and Israel. He also created the forty-day fundraising walk of the entire length of Israel, which raised eighteen thousand dollars for vulnerable kids, and a ten-day Jewish meditation retreat for Israeli backpackers spending time in India. He is now a senior lecturer at Aish HaTorah World Center in Jerusalem, as well as the co-founder/director of Ruach Chayim: Authentic Jewish Meditation Retreats.

Dov Ber is a much sought-after speaker for groups visiting Israel and for shuls and Jewish organizations in the USA, England, South Africa, and Canada. He plans to set up HaGibborim, an organization providing Torah-based personal mastery retreats, as well as longer term programs in Israel, to ensure people are tapping consciously and joyously into the purpose of life and helping others do the same. He lives in Jerusalem with his wife and children.

If you would like to arrange a program with Dov Ber for yourself or your organization, please reach out to him at dovbercohen@gmail.com.

Website: www.dovber.org

Website for his mind, body, soul seminar: www.be-a-master.org

FB page: Peaceful Jewish Warriors

Online shiurim: www.soundcloud.com/dov-ber-cohen

Baghar Orphanage, India, p. 87

Anapurna Mountain Base Camp, Nepal, p. 104

Shaolin kung fu training in Fa Wang Si Temple, China, pp. 92-93